Sense and Certainty

PHILOSOPHICAL THEORY

SERIES EDITORS
John McDowell, Philip Pettit and Crispin Wright

Sense and Certainty
A Dissolution of Scepticism

MARIE McGINN

Basil Blackwell

British Library Cataloguing in Publication Data
McGinn, Marie
Sense and certainty: a dissolution of
scepticism
1. Knowledge. Scepticism
I. Title
121'.5

ISBN 0-631-15786-7

Library of Congress Cataloging in Publication Data
McGinn, Marie.
Sense and certainty.

(Philosophical theory)
Includes index.
1. Skepticism.   I. Title.   II. Series.
BD201.M37 1989   149'.73   88-22207
ISBN 0-631-15786-7

Typeset in 11 on 13pt Baskerville
by Times Graphics
Printed in Great Britain by
T. J. Press (Padstow) Ltd., Padstow, Cornwall

Contents

To my parents

In philosophy we must always ask: 'How must we look at this problem in order for it to become solvable?'

Wittgenstein: *Remarks on Colour*

Preface

I first became interested in the problem of scepticism when I sat in on a seminar given by Thompson Clarke in Berkerley in Autumn Term 1976. Watching him display the unsatisfactoriness of all the familiar arguments against the sceptic, on the one hand, taught me a real respect for the problem, while, on the other hand, his own concern to construct a reply with none of the dogmatic or verificationist defects of the standard arguments had the effect of persuading me that there must be a way out of the muddle. In the following pages I present the reply to the sceptic that I have developed in thinking about the problem more or less continually since I attended Clarke's seminar eleven years ago. The position that I argue for is based on my reading of Wittgenstein's *On Certainty*, but it is at all points influenced by my own sense, derived largely from hearing Thompson Clarke, of what would constitute a satisfactory rebuttal. Other influences that have contributed, either positively or negatively, to the development of my position include Barry Stroud's book, *The Significance of Philosophical Scepticism*, which I heard in draft form in the summer of 1977, Stanley Cavell's *The Claim of Reason*, Michael Williams' *Groundless Belief*, Colin McGinn's *The Subjective View*, and Thomas Nagel's *The View From Nowhere*. For smoothness of presentation, I have not always identified points in the text where what I say is influenced by others, and I should like to take this opportunity to point out that the conception of objectivity presented in chapter 4 is influenced by Colin McGinn, and that the view of the traditional epistemologist developed at the beginning of chapter 7 is influenced by Michael Williams.

I read a draft of the book to a third-year class in Spring Term 1987, and I would like to record my thanks for the large number of useful criticisms that were made. These criticisms were particularly important for my setting out of the sceptical problem in chapter 1, and my discussion of naturalism in chapter 8. I would also like to thank the following people for reading and commenting on an earlier draft: John McDowell, Mark Rowe, Martin Bell, and Richard Francks. Finally, I would like to thank John McDowell, as editor of the series, for inviting me to write a book on scepticism, and for his encouragement at all stages of its development.

Marie McGinn

1

The Problem of Scepticism

This book is concerned with the question whether there is a philosophically satisfactory rebuttal of scepticism. The form of scepticism I am concerned with is scepticism regarding our ability to know about the objective world. It has become increasingly clear to me in thinking about this problem that hope of achieving a resolution of it depends on our first of all becoming clear, not only about the precise form of the sceptic's argument but more generally about the nature of the reflections that precede it and lead to its construction. Certainly, the resolution of the sceptical problem that I develop and defend depends, for whatever conviction it possesses, on the persuasiveness of the conception of scepticism and philosophical reflection that I develop in the course of the book. However, independently of the question whether my suggested resolution is successful, it seems to me that one major advantage of the understanding of what leads to the sceptical conclusion that I offer is that it does indeed make it possible to see how the sceptical problematic could be resolved. On my conception of it, scepticism ceases to be an irritating and perpetual philosophical conundrum, and becomes a problem that emerges for a particular philosophical understanding of the nature of human practice, and thus a problem that may cease to arise for an alternative account.

My discussion of the problem of sceptisicm starts from a point at which the following two facts have already been accepted as incontrovertible:

1 The sceptical argument is both very natural and compelling and completely unanswerable in its own terms: we
   cannot provide the justifications for our knowledge claims
   that the sceptic makes us feel are essential to their being
   correctly sustained.
2 The sceptical conclusion is completely incapable of bringing conviction: we cannot but go on affirming without
   doubt all the judgements that the sceptic's argument
   appear to undermine.

These two facts are, *prima facie*, in profound tension with one
another. The first presses us to accept the sceptic's conclusion
and refrain from all judgements concerning the nature of
reality; the second forces us to acknowledge that we cannot put
off our conviction in the correctness of our world view. Taken
together, the two facts appear to leave us with an unappealing
choice between a philosophical position that is the product of
reason and careful argument but which we cannot for a
moment believe or take seriously, and one that reaffirms our
irresistible common-sense outlook but which has now been
made to look dogmatic and presumptuous. Philosophers have,
I believe, tended to feel rather more comfortable with the
second of these options. But while I agree that a philosophical
position that does not harmonize with the most profound
convictions of our ordinary outlook is deeply unsatisfactory, or
even absurd, I cannot accept that this is enough on its own to
make the bare reaffirmation of common sense a philosophically
satisfactory reply to the sceptic. The question is how can we
achieve a stable, undogmatic position that is not at odds with
our ordinary conviction concerning our ability to know about
the world, once we have acknowledged the impossibility of
providing our view of the world with a rational base?

The first step is, as I just now remarked, to become
absolutely clear about the process by which the sceptic arrives
at an assessment of our ordinary knowledge claims. What I am
concerned with here is not simply to give an account of, say, the
argument of Descartes's *First Meditation*, but rather to offer an
understanding of what is going on when the sceptic is led

irresistibly to the conclusion that we cannot know, or have any reasonable belief about, the objective world. Thus, I want to suggest that it is extremely important that we regard the sceptic as beginning, not with any specific demands concerning the standards of knowledge or reasonable belief, but by taking a reflective attitude towards our practice of making and accepting knowledge claims. He observes that in the course of this practice he has sometimes been forced to accept that he has made false claims to knowledge; that he has, through carelessness or oversight, or through misleading evidence, fallen into error about what is the case. He is therefore led to ask himself whether any among all his current beliefs can be regarded as providing sure and genuine knowledge of reality. Having become thus reflective about our practice, and considering the justifications on the basis of which he accepts a vast number of knowledge claims, the sceptic now observes that these justifications are actually constructed within a framework of judgements that he accepts without doubt, but which can in principle be questioned. Thus, the justifications which he normally accepts as grounding his claims to know about the world all come to a stopping point in judgements that concern either immediately observed facts, or the fact of something's being (having been) observed, or very familiar general beliefs about the world. In the normal way of things, and exceptional circumstances aside, these judgements are never questioned or doubted. Examining them now, the sceptic is forced to acknowledge that they must be regarded as implicit knowledge claims that are open to question and which stand in need of a justification.

The sceptic's procedure is to take a particular instance of a judgement belonging to the framework and see if he can show it to be well-grounded. The sceptic in effect takes a judgement which he would ordinarily regard as part of a completely secure and certain basis for justifying further knowledge claims, and questions whether a claim to know that that judgement itself is true can be given an adequate justification. In so far as the sceptic concerns himself with a particular claim to know, therefore, it is not the sort of claim that we would ordinarily be interested in making, but a claim – 'I know that this is a hand (chair, desk, table, piece of paper, pen, tomato)' – the unquestioned acceptance of which would normally form the backdrop for all enquiry and justification of belief. He looks at this sort of claim, not merely because it represents the 'best case' of a knowledge claim, but because it concerns a sort of judgement that grounds all our further claims to knowledge. It is not only that these judgements appear more certain than any others but also that, given the role they play in the grounding of knowledge claims, if they can't be grounded, then nothing can.

The sceptic's next step is to observe that in order to justify a judgement like 'I know that this is a hand', he would have to show that he possesses evidence for it that is capable of providing it with the necessary support. In order to avoid begging the question at issue, the sceptic must necessarily conceive this evidence in a way that commits him to no claims about the nature of objective reality. It is at this point, therefore, that the idea of evidence that is epistemologically prior to any judgement about the objective world emerges. Thus, the sceptic is led to construct a conception of the evidence for all his knowledge claims that is, in a crucial sense, purely subjective, that is, its description is allowed to incorporate no assumption that this evidence is revelatory of an objective, independent world. What he is led to, in other words, is the idea that his own immediate experience, conceived purely subjectively, must provide the secure, independent base for all his knowledge of reality. His system of beliefs about the objective world will prove well-grounded, therefore, only if the sceptic is able to show that experience, conceived in this purely subjective manner, can support claims about how things stand in objective reality. The sceptic's former acceptance of the objective judgements that formed an unquestioned framework for confirming and disconfirming beliefs must now be supposed to lie on the previously unexamined assumption that experience, in the sense outlined, provides a reliable guide to the nature of reality. Clearly, this makes his former acceptance of these judgements as certain unsatisfactory. If the sceptic is ever to be able to make his acceptance of these judgements look warranted, then he must undertake the task of providing a justification for the unproved (and previously unperceived) assumption that it has hitherto rested on.

The next stage in the sceptic's argument is concerned with the construction of the Sceptical Hypotheses. What the sceptic finds is that he cannot provide the requisite justification for the assumption on which a claim to know a representative judgement of the frame has been found to rest. Thus, far from being able to justify the general principle that experience is a reliable guide to the nature of reality, he finds that he can construct powerful reasons to doubt it. It quickly becomes apparent to the sceptic that there can be nothing in the nature or quality of experience, as he has been led to conceive it, that could itself guarantee that is is of non-delusive origin. No matter how vivid this experience is, and no matter how strong the conviction concerning what is the case that it gives rise to, it cannot be ruled out that the experience itself is merely a form of dream, or that it is induced by some form of evil genius (mad scientist) who causes him to have experiences that are entirely delusive. All attempts to rule out these sceptical alternatives must, the sceptic observes, inevitably depend on treating some experience as a reliable guide to the nature of reality, and hence reason in a circle. Thus he sees that, while there is no doubt about how things appear to him, there are certain hypotheses that account for how things appear which cannot without circularity be ruled out on the basis of how things appear and which prevent him from justifying the general assumption that experience is a reliable guide to the nature of the objective world, which seems to lie behind all the judgements that constitute the ordinary foundation for his system of knowledge.

The sceptic is therefore brought to acknowledge that the general assumption, on which his acceptance of all the judgements that constitute the basis for all further knowledge claims rests, cannot be justified. The project of grounding the ordinary framework judgements, and providing genuine, presupposition-free justifications for his ordinary knowledge claims, has proved incapable of completion. Yet it is clearly unacceptably dogmatic to go back and affirm either the judgements that constitute the framework or the knowledge claims that he bases on them, now that they have all been shown to depend on an unproved, and unprovable, assumption. Before he undertook his reflections, the sceptic supposed himself to be in a position to accept a mass of observational judgements and general beliefs about the world, and to use these in the justification of a very large number of knowledge claims. In the attempt to ground these observational judgements and general beliefs, the sceptic has apparently uncovered an unproved assumption underlying the entire structure, which he cannot justify. He has apparently discovered, therefore, that he is not in a postion to make *any* judgement, either basic or derived, concerning what is the case in reality. All his former framework judgements and all the knowledge claims he based on them should now be suspended or withdrawn.

As I have presented it, then, the process by which the sceptic is led to his conclusion has seven clearly discernible stages:

1 The sceptic takes up a *reflective stance vis-à-vis* our ordinary practice of making and accepting knowledge claims.
2 He observes that he has fallen into error in the past and undertakes the *critical examination* of his current claims to know.
3 He discovers that they are made within a *framework of judgements* which he implicitly claims to know, but which he has never justified.
4 He formulates a *project of justification* regarding the judgements of the frame.
5 He uncovers an *unproved assumption* lying behind his acceptance of the framework judgements.
6 He constructs the *Sceptical Hypotheses* which reveal that the general assumption cannot, without circularity, be justified.
7 He concludes that there should be *complete suspension of judgement* concerning the nature of the objective world.

This formulation of what is going on in the course of the sceptic's reflections is based, in its broad outline, on the argument of Descartes's *First Meditation*. The argument as a whole is, *prima facie*, extremely powerful. It depends, on the one hand, on our accepting the following two claims, both of which seem difficult to deny: first, that all our knowledge claims concerning the nature of reality are supported by justifications which end in judgements which we implicitly claim to know, but the acceptance of which rests on the unproved assumption that experience is a reliable guide to what is the case; second, that the two Sceptical Hypotheses (the dreaming hypothesis and the hypothesis of an evil genius) provide equally adequate accounts of the origin of experience. On the other hand, the argument depends on the following assumptions concerning the concept of knowledge, which appear to be entirely in conformity with our ordinary understanding of that concept: first, that we are in a position to make a claim to know a given proposition only if we possess an adequate justification for believing it to be true; second, that justifications that depend on the acceptance of an unproved assumption are inadequate and unacceptable; and third, that once a justification for a knowledge claim has ben shown to be unacceptable, then that claim, and any futher claim that is based on it, must be withdrawn. *At no point does the argument require us to accept anything that is either obviously false or even open to doubt.*

It is important to observe at this point that the sceptic is here being seen as someone who, employing his ordinary understanding of the concepts of knowledge and justification, undertakes a reflective and critical enquiry into our ordinary practice and our general conviction that we know a great many things. His enquiry does not involve a philosophical definition of the concepts of knowledge and justification, but proceeds purely on the basis of our ordinary understanding of the relation between claiming to know a given proposition and being able to justify it. Furthermore, his enquiry is, on the present account, motivated entirely by the sceptic's ordinary understanding of these two epistemic concepts, and does not arise directly from reflections on the relation between subjective experience and objective reality. The sceptic's concern, in the first instance, is with the question whether our practice is well-grounded, and it is in the course of his reflections on this question that he is led to expose the limitation of the base on which we make objective claims to knowledge. The sceptic is not to be seen as *starting* from a sense that objective reality may be forever beyond his reach, but rather the idea of confinement within experience is something that develops in the course of his reflections. As we have already seen, the first stage in this process involves the sceptic's being led to cast his ordinary framework judgements in the form of knowledge claims. This step sends the sceptic in search of independent evidence that could serve as a secure ground for these claims. This leads, in turn, to the development of a purely subjective conception of experience. Given this conception of experience, our ability to make any judgement concerning the objective world can quickly be made to appear problematic. Thus, we are to see the idea that the sceptic is confined within the perspective of his own subjective experience as something that emerges as a *consequence* of the sceptic's initial assessment of the judgements of the frame as implicit knowledge claims which stand in need of a justification.

If all the above is correct, then its importance lies in the fact that it would seem to indicate that it would be a mistake to focus our attention, in our search for a philosophically satisfactory response to the sceptic, either on a definition of knowledge that will neutralize the force of the sceptic's doubts, or on a definition of objectivity that will secure for us objective knowledge based on experience. What I am suggesting is that *neither the concept of knowledge as such, nor the concept of objectivity as such, represents the real source of the sceptical problem*. It is therefore unlikely that tinkering with either of these concepts offers any hope of a resolution of the problem. The real origin of the problem of scepticism, I am suggesting, lies in the move from our ordinary attitude that regards the judgements of the framework as beyond question, to the belief that they are knowledge claims that stand in need of justifying, And it is to the legitimacy of this move, therefore, that we need to address ourselves. Clearly, this places the current enquiry into scepticism in opposition to two well-established trends in recent epistomology, and I shall have occasion to say something more about these trends in following chapters.

I have presented the sceptic's argument in a way that both brings out the structure of the sceptic's reflections and reveals them as philosophically immensely compelling. Yet it is also an extremely important fact about scepticism that, despite its philosophical cogency, it is completely without power to bring about the suspension of judgement that it seems to demand. Thus, for example, we find that Descartes, having constructed the sceptical argument in the *First Meditation*, finds himself constrained to confess that it is completely incapable of persuading him to put off conviction and abandon his ordinary outlook. He writes as follows:

> But [the] task [of suspending judgement] is a laborious one, and *insensibly a certain lassitude leads me into the course of my ordinary life.* And just as a captive who in sleep enjoys an imaginary liberty, when he begins to suspect that his liberty is but a dream, fears to awaken, and conspires with these agreeable illusions that the deception may be prolonged, *so insensibly and of my own accord I fall back into my former opinions,* and I dread waking from this slumber, lest the laborious wakefulness which would follow the tranquility of this repose should have to be spent not in daylight, but in the excessive darkness of the difficulties which have just been discussed. (pp. 148–9, my italics)

Thus whatever conviction the sceptic's conclusion possesses while we are in the reflective stance that characterizes the sceptic's enquiry, it is entirely lost when we revert to the natural standpoint of common sense. The sceptic's conclusion is quite unable to detach itself from the reflective perspective that revealed it and enter into our lives as a practical lived conviction. The tension between the sceptic's conclusion and our ordinary assessment of judgements and knowledge claims is not, therefore, a tension between two arguments with contradictory conclusions, which can be appreciated from a single perspective. The emergence of the tension between scepticism and ordinary life depends on the adoption of two entirely different perspectives which yield profoundly conflicting conceptions of our ordinary practice. The conflict is between how things present themselves from an engaged perspective, or the standpoint of common sense, and how they present themselves when looked at reflectively, from a detached or philosophical point of view. The philosopher's assessment of the framework judgements as presumptous and in need of a justification that cannot in fact be given, is simply not one that can be felt or taken seriously by someone who is engaged in ordinary practice. Philosophical doubt and common-sense conviction are attitudes that appear only with the adoption of the appropriate perspective: live and be convinced; reflect and doubt. These two positions represent mutually exclusive alternatives.

The inability of the sceptic's argument to prevent him from taking up his former judgements and opinions as soon as his philosophical reflections cease is not something that delays or becomes a matter of real concern for Descartes. And it is not difficult to see why. For Descartes , unlike the Ancient Sceptics, does not construct the sceptical argument as a preliminary to describing a life without belief. Rather, Descartes intends to use the sceptical argument to reveal a system of beliefs based, not on sensory experience, but on clear and distinct perception and entirely immune to sceptical doubt. The intellectual grounds for doubting his former judgements and beliefs which he has formulated represent only a *temporary stage* in an overall project that will return us ultimately to rationally justified knowledge of reality. The role of sceptical doubt in Descartes's overall project does not require him to show that the sceptical conclusion can seriously be lived; the sceptical conclusion does not provide the stopping point for his reflections. Sceptical doubt is merely a tool which uncovers, on the one hand, our initial inability to justify any claim to knowledge of reality on the basis of experience, and on the other, our possession of a faculty (clear and distinct perception) which, when properly employed, yields knowledge that is supported by genuine, presupposition-free justifications. For Descartes, our inability to live scepticism is entirely unimportant, since he believes that conviction in our knowledge of the external world is something that can be achieved from within the reflective stance of philosophy. The sceptical argument can therefore play its role without it ever becoming necessary to address the problem of the tension between the sceptic's conclusion and our ordinary unshakeable conviction that we know a great deal about the world.

However, I am taking it as an initial assumption that we can no longer regard ourselves as being in the same happy position as Descartes. Doubt has now become intrinsic to the philosophical stance. We cannot hope to justify our conception of the world, either on the basis of experience or on the basis of reason; justifications for the judgements that form the framework of our practice are simply unavailable. We cannot, therfore, regard the sceptical conclusion as a mere temporary stopping point in a philosophical project that will ultimately justify our world view, but must confront it in the form of a problematic that reveals to us our inability to justify a conception that we cannot put off or distance ourselves from, but which continues to inspire our complete and unqualified conviction. We are no longer looking for a *solution* to the sceptic's difficulties; that is to say, we are not attempting to bring philosophy and common sense into harmony by providing the justifications that the sceptic believes are needed. Our question is, rather, whether we can achieve harmony by constructing a philosophical understanding of the judgements of the framework that allows us to see why the absence of justification here does not have the consequences the sceptic believes it has. What we want is a philosophical account of ordinary practice that does not generate a conclusion that is in conflict with our ordinary common-sense outlook. The question is whether ordinary practice can be revealed, from within a philosophical perspective, as something that is *both* ungrounded *and* non-presumptuous.

The discussion of this question will focus on the work of four philosophers – Moore, Austin, Stanley Cavell and Wittgenstein. All four philosophers share my general assumption that the justification for our world view that the sceptic believes is needed cannot be provided and that his negative conclusion is, in an absolutely strict sense, beyond belief. Moreover, all four share the view that a satisfactory response to scepticism does justice to its complete unliveability only if it yields a defence of common sense that does not involve any form of philosophical qualification or dilution of our ordinary knowledge claims.

Thus, all four believe that the tension between philosophical doubt and ordinary life cannot be resolved by giving a philosophical interpretation of our ordinary knowledge claims, which construes them idealistically or as concerned with something other than objective truth (e.g. expediency). Whatever philosophical understanding of ordinary practice we achieve, it is generally agreed that it is satisfactory only if it is in harmony with common sense's own robust conception of itself. That is to say, a philosophically adequate resolution of our problematic must preserve the position that we hold at the outset, viz. that our ordinary knowledge claims are largely true, and concern a mind-independent, verification-transcendent reality.

The major difficulty for any approach that sets out to give a philosophical defence of unqualified common sense, without providing a rational grounding for the judgements that form its frame, is, plainly, to avoid becoming merely dogmatic, and simply re-affirming our right to the judgements and knowledge claims that the sceptic appears to show we ought not to make. Any philosophical response that tries to use the power of our ordinary conviction as on its own a basis for rejecting the sceptic's conclusison can never be fully satisfactory. We do not resolve the tension between the two perspectives simply by affirming the correctness of what is revealed from one of them. The unliveability of scepticism does not on its own provide a proper philosophical basis for rejecting or neglecting the sceptical problematic. Moreover, the objection to a dogmatic rejection of scepticism is not merely that it is dogmatic, but that it fails to provide any understanding of the significance of the fact that we cannot justify a conception of the world that we all accept without doubt. The philosophical understanding of ordinary practice that is to allow us to see the latter as both ungrounded and non-presumptuous has simply not been provided by a philosophical position that offers common sense itself as the answer to scepticism.

A philosophically satisfactorily resolution of our problematic requires, therefore, that the view of ordinary practice from the engaged perspective and the view from the philosophical perspective become genuinely unified. *Philosophy must no longer undermine common sense and common sense must no longer falsify philosophy.* We require, in other words, a philosophy that does justice to both the unliveability and the unanswerability of scepticism. It must allow the absence of a justification for the judgements that form the frame of our practice to reveal something significant about these judgements, but in such a way that it no longer prompts the sceptical conclusion. By the same token, it must allow our ordinary conviction in these judgements to emerge as something that is neither presumptuous nor dogmatic; it must allow us to see our conviction as legitimate even though it lacks a rational base. Such a non-sceptical philosophical understanding of ordinary practice would no longer require us to betray our lived conviction in our world view in a philosophical doctrine that denies us unqualified knowledge of reality. At the same time, it would enable us to avoid dogmatism and understand the significance of the fact that we cannot, in a certain strict sense, justify our view of the world.

2

The Conflict between Scepticism and Common Sense

Before I begin discussing the question whether any of our four philosophers – Moore, Austin, Cavell and Wittgenstein – provides a satisfactory philosophical response to the sceptic, I want to spend some time considering how we should conceive of the relationship between the sceptical reflections I have described, with their negative conclusion, and our ordinary practice of claiming to know things. My account of the nature of the sceptic's reflections already makes it clear that I believe that scepticism starts in the adoption of a comtemplative stance that examines human knowledge *as a whole*. In this respect, the sceptic's investigation of knowledge is quite different from the sort of enquiries concerning *particular knowledge claims* that we undertake within our ordinary practice. Thus, while the sceptic may appear, in stages 4 and 5 (see p. 6 above) of his enquiry, to investigate a particular knowledge claim (e.g. 'I know that this is a hand'), the preliminaries to his investigation of this claim (i.e. stages 1–3, p. 6) show that it is functioning quite differently from an ordinary knowledge claim, made in the context of ordinary life. First of all, because the sceptic is concerned with our justification for affirming the judgements that normally form the frame of our practice, the claim is of a sort that we would never normally make or be interested in.

Second, the claim that the sceptic selects is, to a certain extent, arbitrary, for it is really functioning as a representative of the frame as a whole; he uses it ultimately in order to discover whether he can ground the general assumption, common to all judgements of the frame, that experience provides a reliable guide to the nature of reality. The sceptic's claim functions, therefore, as a focus of attention for a doubt that really afflicts our entire system of knowledge, and not just the particular claim that is being investigated. It is, of course, because of these features of his enquiry that the conclusion the sceptic is led to draw relates, not only to the particular claim investigated, but to all our judgements and claims concerning the nature of reality.

Scepticism is remote from ordinary practice in another sense as well. In acknowledging that sceptisicm is unliveable, we are implicitly accepting that the doubt concerning our framework judgements, on the basis of which the sceptic criticizes our ordinary knowledge claims, could never be felt as a real doubt, as a doubt that might seriously be entered in a practical or lived context. Thus, while the sceptic can, from the reflective stance, make the judgements of the frame appear presumptuous, dependent on the unproved assumption of the reliability of experience, we can never really *feel* them as presumptuous, or perceive them, from a lived point of view, as dependent on any assumption whatever. The sceptic's view of the judgements of the frame, his doubts, and his negative conclusion, are, as I observed in chapter 1, confined to the special reflective stance that I have identified as stage 1 (p. 6) of his argument.

However, while there are these striking differences between the sceptic's enquiry and an ordinary enquiry, between the sceptic's doubt and the sort of doubt that might be felt in everyday life, it nevertheless appears to be the case that the enquiry, the doubts, and the conclusion the sceptic draws, all relate to the very judgements and knowledge claims that we affirm or accept in a practical context. The sceptic's enquiry is special in all the ways I have outlined, but it still concerns *our* system of judgements and *our* knowledge claims, and not some philosophical counterparts of these. The sceptic at least does not appear to begin his enquiry by changing what is meant by 'know', or by upping the standard of what counts as an adequate justification for a knowledge claim. On the face of it, what the sceptic's enquiry leads him to discover is something that our ordinary grasp of epistemic concepts allows us to see is a weakness in the justifications that ground our ordinary knowledge claims. He shows that all our ordinary justifications depend on judgements that depend on an unproved assumption that cannot be justified. Our ordinary understanding of the epistemic concepts involved seems to oblige us to concede that this is inadequate. We cannot but recognize, it seems, that our ordinary knowledge claims and the judgements they rest on are not well-grounded, and that all of them should be suspended or withdrawn. And this is, of course, in outright conflict with our ordinary practical propensity to accept a mass of judgements concerning external facts and derive justifications for a mass of further knowledge claims from them. On this view of matters, the tension between the unanswerability of scepticism and its unliveability is maximal. The attitude of common sense and the revelations of philosophical contemplation are in diametric opposition. Common sense affirms and accepts as true the very judgements and claims that philosophy shows ought never to be made or accepted.

In his book, *The Significance of Philosophical Scepticism*, Barry Stroud attempts to articulate and defend a different conception of the relation between philosophical scepticism and common sense. Stroud believes that as long as we regard the relation between scepticism and common sense in the way I have just described, then we are forced to accept that only one of them can provide the correct description of our right, or otherwise, to affirm and accept knowledge claims. But in that case, he believes, the hold that our familiar assessments have on us, and our failure to enter, or feel any force in, sceptical objections to knowledge claims made in a practical context may easily incline us to a hasty dismissal of the sceptic. Thus, keeping our eye firmly on our ordinary assessments of knowledge claims, we might suppose that the sceptic comes to his pessimistic conclusion only because his reflective stance causes him to make subtle alterations in the concept of knowledge, and to set the standard for what counts as knowing what is the case in external reality much too high. Stroud writes:

> as soon as we even glance in the direction of the standards and procedures we follow in everyday life we will find that there is nothing at all in Descartes's argument. It is obvious that we do not always insist that people know that they are not dreaming before we allow that they know something in everyday life, or even in science or a court of law, where the standards are presumably much stricter. So it can easily look as if Descartes reaches his sceptical conclusion only by violating our ordinary standards and requirements for knowledge, perhaps substituting a new and different set of his own. (ibid., pp. 39–40)

Stroud, of course, is anxious that no such easy dismissal of the sceptic's reasoning should be possible. His own sense is that the problem of scepticism raises much deeper philosophical issues than that for which the above quick rebuttal allows. He therefore undertakes the task of showing how we can both see the sceptic as operating with our ordinary concept of knowledge and yet put off any obviously unreasonable consequences of his argument. Thus he sets out to show that the sceptic's negative conclusion is not actually in conflict with out right to affirm all our ordinary claims to know about the world. Stroud starts from our acknowledged sense that sceptical doubt is completely remote from ordinary practice, and argues that, although the sceptic is employing all our ordinary concepts, he is operating within a realm of discourse – philosophy – from which our ordinary assertions are *insulated*. Stroud's aim is to provide a sphere of operation for the philosophical sceptic, in which he can compete equally with alternative philosophical descriptions of our epistemic position, without prejudice from our propensity, in a practical context, to regard ourselves as in a position to sustain knowledge claims concerning external facts, and without fear of the charge of irrelevance to our ordinary practice of claiming to know things. What he tries to show is that, despite the fact that the same concept of knowledge is being employed in both the philosophical and the common-sense stance, and despite the fact that they appear to make quite different assessments of our right to make assertions involving it, scepticism and common sense, or ordinary practice, are not strictly in conflict with one another.

On Stroud's rendering of the sceptical argument, the sceptic spends little time in preliminaries but rather moves straight to the investigation of a knowledge claim. The peculiarities of the philosophical realm of discourse are seen as allowing the sceptic to discover, as it were for the first time, that in order to establish his claim to know he must be in a position to know that he is not dreaming. Indeed, he is led to discover that he is *always* in this position, and that in order for him, or for *any of us*, to know *anything* about the world, we must have it in our power to establish that we are not dreaming. However, because the possibility that we are dreaming can perpetually recur to undermine any claim to know that we are not dreaming, the sceptic immediately realizes that the condition on knowledge that he has uncovered can never be fulfilled. Thus, the sceptical argument, on Stroud's view of it, turns on a discovery about the concept of knowledge, or about the conditions for knowing, that shows that we are never in a postion to know anything about the world. The sceptic doesn't use our ordinary concept of knowledge unreflectively and discover a hitherto unperceived inadequacy in our system of judgements and knowledge claims. Rather, he brings to our awareness a hitherto unperceived condition on our possessing knowledge of the world, in order to reveal to us that we can never in fact achieve a state of knowledge.

By contrast with what the philosopher discovers about our concept of knowledge, Stroud believes that our ordinary employment of the words 'I know' is such that we regard a knowledge claim as undermined *only* by doubts that are based on possibilities which there is *some special reason* to think might actually obtain. Thus, in a practical context, if there is no special reason to suppose I might be dreaming, then I do not have to rule out the dream-possibility in order correctly to claim to know something about the external world. The conditions for knowledge that we ordinarily operate with are ones that we frequently fulfil satisfactorily. In order to put off the hasty dismissal of the sceptic's conclusion, Stroud attempts to develop an understanding of the relationship between philosophy and common sense on which it may, on the one hand, be allowed that our ordinary use of the words 'I know' is entirely legitimate, and on the other, on which it may still be maintained that the sceptic's description of the conditions for knowledge is correct, and his pessimistic conclusion on the possibility of knowledge the only one that can justifiably be held. Stroud's development of this idea has a weak version and a strong version. I shall discuss the weak version first.

On Stroud's weak version of the idea that ordinary practice is insulated from any practical effect of a doctrine of philosophical scepticism, there is no suggestion that our ordinary knowledge claims could be *true* at the same time as the sceptic's conclusion. The claim is, rather, that the truth of the sceptical conclusion is compatible with our ordinary use of the words 'I know' being entirely 'reasonable' or 'appropriate'; that is, it is held that all our ordinary knowledge claims could be quite correctly made, even though they are all strictly speaking false. Stroud's idea is that the conditions under which a claim of the form *I know p*, for a given proposition p, is *true*, and the conditions under which it is *justifiably asserted* may come apart. In particular, the conditions of justifiable assertion may be fulfilled, even though the truth-conditions fail to obtain. Stroud argues that the connection between assertion, belief, and action could make it expedient, in practical circumstances, to employ assertability-conditions that are in this sense logically independent of truth-conditions. Thus, in ordinary life, where we operate under the perpetual constraint of the practical need to act, it may be expedient to enter and act on knowledge claims that are supported by justifications that fail to reach the standard that is required for the strict truth of the claim. The conditions under which, in a practical context, we are correct (or justified) in making a claim to know p could, in that case, be correctly described by the weaker condition set out above, while the strict truth of the claim requires fulfilment of the conditions set out by the sceptic:

> On the conception I have in mind, the requirement that there must be some 'special reason' for thinking a certain

possibility might obtain in order for that possibility to be relevant to a particular knowledge-claim would be seen as a requirement on the appropriate or reasonable assertion of knowledge, but not necessarily as a requirement on knowledge itself. In the absence of such a 'special reason', one might perhaps be fully justified in saying 'I know that p' even though it is not true that one knows p. Descartes reaches his sceptical conclusion about our knowledge of the world around us on the basis of a condition he holds to be necessary for the truth of 'I know that p'. (Ibid., p. 63).

Stroud believes that the facts of ordinary usage cannot on their own falsify the claim that they reflect the conditions under which a knowledge claim is justifiably assertible, and that the conditions for genuine knowledge are as described by the sceptic. His suggestion for how the sceptic may preserve ordinary usage while insisting on the correctness of his own assessment of knowledge is, he believes, to this extent satisfactory. He believes, furthermore, that there are important philosophical considerations which ought to make this conception of ordinary practice and its relation to philosophical scepticism highly attractive to us. For it does, he argues, express a conception of *objectivity*, and of what it is to stand in a relation of knowledge to the external world, that is deeply entrenched in human thought and cannot easily be abandoned. Thus, the philosophical sceptic, it is held, may lend colour to the idea that ordinary practice is governed by a restriction of expediency, and that his own analysis sets out what is really requisite for knowledge, by appeal to the conception of objectivity that the latter allegedly embodies, and which we cannot readily disown.

Stroud describes this conception of objectivity as follows:

I am trying to express a conception of the independence of the world, of the idea that the world is there quite independently of human knowledge and belief, that I think we all understand. It embodies a conception of objectivity, of things being a certain way whether anyone is affected by them or interested in them or knows or believes anything about them or not. There seems to be nothing in the conception itself to imply that knowledge or reasonable belief about the external world is impossible . . . What we want to find out . . . is what is true, what the objective facts of the matter are. And what we aspire to and eventually claim to know is the objective truth or falsity of (a given proposition) . . . What we aspire to and eventually claim to know is something that holds quite independently of our knowing it or of our being in a position reasonably to assert it. That is the very idea of objectivity. (Ibid., p. 78).

Stroud's claim, then, is that this conception of the objectivity of the objects of human knowledge is one that we cannot but acknowledge that we share with the sceptic. It consists, he says, in 'nothing more than the merest platitudes' (ibid., p. 76), and we cannot convincingly deny that it captures the very essence of our ordinary understanding. But now, Stroud argues, we must also agree that whether anyone ever does know anything about the world is itself a question of objective fact, a question altogether independent of whether we ever do, for practical purposes, regard ourselves as in a position to affirm knowledge of reality. Knowing about the world is a matter of standing in a certain sort of objective relation to an independent reality. It is a state which, through a practical indifference to objective truth, we could be wrong in attributing to ourselves. Truth-conditions and assertibility-conditions may come apart. In ordinary life we are concerned with the purely practical question of whether we are, for practical purposes, justified in *acting as if* we had knowledge of reality. The sceptic, on the other hand, is concerned purely with the question whether we ever really do know what is the case; that is, whether we ever do stand in that objective relation to reality objectively conceived. What the sceptic seeks is

a certain kind of understanding of our state or our relation to the facts – what might be called an objective understanding of our position. Whether someone (even ourselves) knows a certain thing is . . . [an] objective matter of fact . . . and what we seek is knowledge of whether or not that objective matter obtains, and perhaps in addition some understanding of how the conditions necessary and sufficient for its obtaining have been fulfilled. (Ibid., pp. 79–80).

The philosophical stance of the sceptic is thus conceived as one in which he puts off the practical concerns of ordinary life and applies himself purely disinterestedly to the question whether the conditions for the truth of a claim to know external facts are ever met. Our ordinary claims to know about reality are seen as attributing to us a type of objective relation to the world, which itself invites us to put off our practical concerns and question ourselves disinterestedly (or philosophically) as to whether we ever really do know. Thus, while we are ordinarily interested in what we can, for practical purposes, claim to know, our understanding of what our claim is aiming at already suggests the possibility of another enquiry (a philosophical enquiry) into whether the claim is ever really *true*. In this way, Stroud seeks at once to motivate the sceptic's enquiry, and at the same time, to preserve our ordinary practice of making and accepting knowledge claims from any revisionary consquences of its outcome. We have a conception of knowledge which obliges us to acknowledge the independence of the truth of knowledge claims from their assertability in practical contexts. The interest of the question whether the truth-conditions of our own concept of knowledge are ever fulfilled is, Stroud believes, manifest. Yet the practical concerns of ordinary life are on their own sufficient to warrant our continuing to operate with assertability-conditions that are logically independent of truth-conditions, whatever the outcome of the disinterested philosophical enquiry should be. On this version of the insulation doctrine, Stroud preserves scepticism from the threat posed by the grip of ordinary practice, by motivating the idea that philosophical contemplation could reveal that all our ordinary knowledge claims are false, and yet pragmatic constraints on ordinary practice make it quite correct to say, in the sort of circumstances we do say, that we know external facts.

At the beginning of this chapter I suggested that our initial intuition is that the conclusion of the sceptic and the claims of common sense are in outright conflict with one another. Stroud has now developed an understanding of the sceptic's enquiry on which there is a sort of compatibility between them. The truth of the sceptic's conclusion is not compatible with the truth of our ordinary claims, but it is compatible with its being correct to go on making them. The question is whether this view of the relationship between the conclusion concerning our epistemic position that we reach while in the reflective stance, and our ordinary practice of affirming knowledge claims, really makes sense. Can we really make sense of the idea that our ordinary knowledge claims could be quite correctly made and none the less, for the sorts of reasons the sceptic advances, be false? I will argue that we cannot. Not because I wish to put forward the sort of hasty dismissal of scepticism that Stroud is anxious to undercut, but merely because I want to defend the view that our initial intuition that the sceptic's assessment of ordinary practice is in outright conflict with our engaged assessment of it is correct.

Stroud defends his view of the relationship between philosophical scepticism and common sense by pointing out that the distinction between its being true that one knows a given proposition, p, and its being correct to say that one knows p is one that we frequently make in the course of ordinary practice. Stroud imagines a case (ibid., pp. 58–61) in which we have maximally good grounds for making a claim to know a proposition, p, and in which, through some completely unforeseeable circumstances, p turns out to be false. In such a case, Stroud observes, we would regard the claim to know p as strictly false, but still consider the original claim to have been quite correctly made. Thus, we have something that looks rather like the sort of distinction Stroud employs in his characterization of the relationship between scepticism and common sense: The claim to know p is quite correct or beyond criticism, yet the claim itself is strictly speaking a false one. However, the distinction as it crops up here is not being used in quite the same way as it is in Stroud's account. In the current case, the distinction between the claim's being true and its being correct to make the claim depends on its turning out later that the propositional content of the claim is actually false. At no point is there any suggestion that there is some defect in the *grounds* on the basis of which the claim was originally made; within an ordinary context these grounds constitute just the sort of grounds capable of supporting a claim to know the embedded proposition, and in the course of the description of the example nothing occurs to bring the grounds under scrutiny or suspicion. The original claim remains correct, even though it turns out to be false, precisely because we continue to see the original grounds as entirely adequate.

By contrast, Stroud needs to employ the distinction in cases where the falsity of the claim arises, not because the embedded propositions are false, but because the justifications on which the claims are based do not reach the standard requisite for knowledge. Stroud, indeed, concedes this point, but he argues that the distinction between strict truth and justified assertion can also be employed in this second sort of case, to show how the falsity of the claim may still leave it beyond criticism. He writes:

> My failure to know in [the first sort of] case as originally described was due to the falsity of what I claimed to know. That necessary condition of knowledge was unfulfilled even though no one at the time was in a position to know that it was unfulfilled, and no one at the time was in a position appropriately or reasonably to criticize my claim on that basis. Perhaps the same is true of other necessary conditions of knowledge. (Ibid., pp. 60–61)

Stroud now goes on to imagine a variation on the first sort of case. We are to suppose that when the claim to know p is originally entered, someone objects to it on the grounds that some extremely improbable possibility – say, the one that does actually obtain and make p false – has not been ruled out. Stroud suggests that the objection is quite plainly, in this practical context, 'outrageous'. However, he argues that it does not follow from this that my ruling out [this bizarre possibility] is simply *not* a condition of my knowing [p]. Its being a necessary condition of my knowledge is so far at least compatible with [the objection's] being inappropriate or outrageous ... A necessary condition of knowledge might remain unfulfilled even though it would be outrageous for anyone to assert that it is or inappropriate for anyone to criticize my knowledge-claim on that basis. The inappropriateness or outrageousness might have some source other than the falsity of what is said or implied about knowledge. (Ibid., p. 62)

The alternative possible source of the 'outrageousness' is, of course, the conditions that govern what it is, on the grounds of expediency, correct to say in a practical context. Stroud concludes his attempt to extend the distinction between truth and justified assertion to this new sort of case as follows:

If it is possible for the conditions sufficient for appropriate or reasonable utterance to be fulfilled even though what is said is not literally true – and it does seem that it is possible – someone might be fully justified in saying he knows some particular thing about the world without its being true that he does know that thing. In particular, when someone claims to know something about the world without asking himself or even thinking of a certain possibility, and that possibility, if realised, would mean that he does not know what he claims to know, he might fail to know in that situation precisely because he has not eliminated that possibility. If there were no special reason for him to consider that possibility, he might nevertheless be fully justified in saying he knows. (Ibid., p. 63)

I think it is impossible to feel at all happy with this. There are, it seems to me, at least two grounds for unease. First of all, there appears to be a crucial difference between the two types of case at the time the original claim is made. There is an important difference in the relationship between the two sorts of failure of truth-conditions of *I know p* and the conditions for its correct assertion. What I want to argue is that there is nothing in ordinary practice to suggest that we would tolerate the idea that the justification for a knowledge claim might be defective and the claim be quite correctly made. Second, there is even more profound ground for unease when we begin to look at both sorts of failure of truth-condition from the point of view of a time when the failure to meet the necessary condition for knowledge has actually been discovered and pointed out. Thus, there is nothing in ordinary practice to suggest that *known* failures of conditions necessary for knowledge are compatible with its being correct to go on making the claim. The conclusion I want ultimately to draw is that the principles of ordinary practice itself require that if the sceptic has really uncovered a defect in our justifications for our framework judgements and the claims that we base on them, then this does indeed reveal that these judgements and claims are not warranted and should be withdrawn.

Let us look at the first of these two grounds for unease in more detail. Imagine that in an ordinary practical context a claim to know a given proposition, p, is entered at a time, t. We have agreed that if p is, through some unforeseeable circumstance, false at t, then the claim to know p is false at t, even though it might be quite correctly made at t. Stroud also wants us to accept that it is in conformity with our ordinary understanding of how the concept of knowledge is employed, that we could possess only an incomplete justification for believing p at t, so that the claim to know p is false at t, but again the claim may still be quite correctly made at t. Yet it seems to me that a crucial difference between the two sorts of necessary condition for knowledge makes it impossible to suppose that our ordinary understanding of what it is to be in a position to claim to know something, permits us to draw a distinction between truth and justified assertion in the second sort of case.

The truth of p is an *objective* condition of knowledge; that is, a condition such that its obtaining or not is independent of our knowing whether or not it obtains. The truth of p cannot, therefore, be part of the grounds for asserting that I know p, although it is a condition for the truth of the assertion. If the grounds for asserting that I know p are met (if I believe p and can justify my believing p), and if the objective condition also obtains (if p is true), then the claim that I know p is also true. However, it is clear that the first two conditions might be met and yet the third should not obtain; it is possible to have justified false beliefs. It is for precisely this reason that claims to know p can fail, while the claim to believe p cannot. Possessing a non-defective justification for believing p is not, however, objective in the same sense. Whether a justification for a knowledge claim is adequate or defective – e.g., whether it imports an unproved assumption, or employs a falsehood, or depends on faulty reasoning – is something that is discoverable (disability aside) from a careful scrutiny of the justification itself. That the justification for a claim to know p is not defective in any of these, or in any other, ways is, therefore, what it means to possess an adequate justification for believing p, and part of the condition for the correct assertion of the knowledge claim. Possession of an adequate or non-defective justification is, in other words, not only part of the truth-conditions of a claim to know p, but also part of its assertability-conditions. If a claim to know p is made in a case where the justification is defective in some way, then, at the time that it is made, it is not only false but incorrect.

It seems to me, therefore, that it is part of our ordinary understanding of the concept of knowledge that possession of an adequate or non-defective justification for believing p is a condition for the correct assertion of the claim to know p. There is simply no room for the idea that the justification for believing p may suffer from some defect, but expediency might make a claim to know p legitimate. It follows that if the sceptic is correct in assessing the principle that experience is a reliable guide to the nature of reality as an unproved assumption lying behind our entire system of knowledge claims, then, in so far as this is a defect, he has shown that we do not possess adequate justifications for any of our claims, and that they are therefore incorrect. It is true, of course, that we are only able to per-ceive the defect as a defect from the reflective stance of philosophy, and that from within our engaged position we are quite unable to take the sceptic's assessment seriously. However, that is only to acknowledge the profound conflict between how matters present themselves to the two perspectives. It need not prompt us to deny the fact that the philosophical assessment appears to pinpoint a sort of defect in our justifications for our ordinary knowledge claims that, on our ordinary understanding of the grounds for asserting such claims, makes all of them unwarranted or incorrect.

If we turn now to the second source of unease, the difficulty for Stroud's attempt to make ordinary practice compatible with the truth of philosophical scepticism becomes still more apparent. For it seems clear that, in both the first and the second sort of case, once the failure of the necessary condition for knowledge has actually been discovered and pointed out, whatever the correctness or incorrectness of the original claim, any current claim to know must at this point be withdrawn. Thus, in the first sort of case, it is plain that once it is discovered that p is false, the claim to know p can no longer be correctly made. And it seems equally plain that once a defect in our justification for a claim to know p is pointed out, the defect must either be corrected or withdrawn. There is absolutely no evidence from ordinary practice that the distinction between truth and justified assertion is ever applied to a knowledge claim made after the failure of truth-condition has been established. And again, this suggests that, whatever we say about our position before the sceptic constructs his argument, our position now that it has been constructed is as follows. If the sceptic has really uncovered a genuine defect in the justifications for our ordinary knowledge claims, and if that defect cannot be corrected, then, by the principles of ordinary practice, we ought not to go on claiming to know external facts.

I do not, of course, wish to deny that if we imagine the sceptic's criticisms of our justifications for our ordinary knowledge claims being made in a practical context, then they would be rejected out of hand. I have already accepted as much by allowing that sceptical doubt is restricted to the philosophical perspective, that it is strictly unliveable, and that it is quite incapable of undermining our lived conviction in the correctness of our ordinary world view. However, I am arguing that the workings of ordinary practice, or the principles for asserting and continuing to assert knowledge claims, make it impossible to accept the interpretation that Stroud is attempting to impose on this fact. Given the relation between justification and assertability-conditions, and given that known failures of necessary conditions for knowledge forthwith undermine a claim, there is simply no room for the idea that the sceptic could show all our ordinary claims to be unjustified and therefore false, but that it could still be quite correct for us to go on making them. It seems, therefore, that as long as we are in a position of having to accept that the sceptic does indeed uncover a defect in our justifications for our ordinary knowledge claims, then we cannot escape the conclusion that he has shown that these claims ought not to be made. Our lived conviction in our world view makes it impossible to rest content with this, but I believe that Stroud's attempt to reduce the tension, by trying to make ordinary practice compatible with the sceptic's assessment, is, on this version anyway, unconvincing and misguided.

I made it clear at the outset that Stroud's view of the relationship between scepticism and common sense is aimed at vindicating the sceptic in the face of a certain hasty dismissal that might be prompted by our inability to take sceptical doubt seriously in a practical or lived context. It is perhaps worth remarking, therefore, that the account of the relationship between scepticism and everyday life that we have just been discussing is vulnerable in precisely the same way. For it seems clear that as soon as we take up our everyday stance, we cannot take seriously the idea that all our ordinary knowledge claims are strictly speaking false, and may be entered on grounds of expediency. The idea of literal falsehood and practical expediency is as impossible to make one's own as the original straightforward sceptical conclusion. Thus, 'as soon as we even glance in the direction of the standards and procedures we follow in everyday life we will find that there is nothing at all' in the idea that we do not *really* know, but are only *saying* that we do. Our absolute conviction regarding our world-view and the knowledge claims that are made within it is simply incapable of being qualified in the way Stroud's weaker version of the relationship between scepticism and common sense requires.

In the end, Stroud himself appears to be dissatisfied with this version of the relationship between scepticism and common sense. For although he believes that the above account achieves a sort of immunity for our ordinary knowledge claims from any revisionary consequences of scepticism, it still remains a fact that, on this account, the *truth* of our knowledge claims is in conflict with the *truth* of the sceptic's conclusion. Stroud seems to believe that in so far as this is true, he has not yet established a sufficient degree of remoteness between philosophical scepticism and ordinary practice. He suggests that it is our undeniable sense that, on the one hand, an ordinary claim to know, in ideal circumstances, say, that the object before one is a hand is not only legitimate but actually *true*, and on the other, that the truth of this claim is *not* a refutation of the philosophical sceptic's argument to show that we cannot know external facts. If we are to understand both the power of the sceptic's reasoning and its inability to touch ordinary practice, then, Stroud believes, we must construe the relationship between the two in such a way that the actual *truth* of our ordinary assessments is compatible with the *truth* of the sceptical conclusion. He believes that this task of completely separating the philosophical assessment of knowledge from our ordinary assessment of it is an essential preliminary to any philosophical resolution of the problem of scepticism. It means understanding why the philosophical sceptic is not refuted by the obvious truth of the ordinary claim ' I know that this is a hand', and it offers a hope of seeing what is required to unravel the riddle of scepticism.

The stronger version of the doctrine that ordinary practice is insulated from scepticism that Stroud articulates attempts, therefore, to regard the truth of the sceptic's conclusion (or of any other philosophical assessment of human knowledge) as compatible, not merely with the 'correctness' of our ordinary knowledge claims, but with their truth. The basis of this second version of the relationship between philosophy and ordinary life is an alleged distinction between two ways of speaking or employing our words. On the one hand, there is the *empirical*, or *internal*, or *plain* way of speaking (the employment of words in ordinary practice), and on the other, there is the *transcendental*, or *external*, or *philosophical* way of speaking (the employment of words within philosophical discourse). Stroud's attitude towards the transcendental or philosophical realm is ambivalent. On the one hand, he appears to believe that one of the most promising lines of attack against scepticism is to try to show that this mode of employing words is not fully intelligible. On the other hand, he feels himself perpetually drawn to acknowledge that he does at least appear to understand the sceptic's use of our language. Not only that, but he cannot escape the feeling that the philosophical enquiry that the sceptic undertakes considers human knowledge from the intellectually important 'objective perspective' which was introduced in the course of motivating the weaker version of the insulation doctrine. For Stroud, the *depth* of the issue raised by scepticism lies precisely in the fact that it forces us to question whether this conception of objectivity, and of an objective understanding of our epistemic position, which underpins it, is really coherent.

Stroud's argument for the claim that philosophy and ordinary practice constitute two distinct areas of discourse turns largely on the point that when someone makes a claim to know, say, that he is not dreaming, in an ordinary practical context, sceptical doubts about the ground for his claim are completely out of place and may simply be dismissed. Yet when the very same claim is made (e.g. by Descartes) in a philosophical context, the sceptic's doubts are both relevant and apparently fatal to our ability to sustain the claim. He illustrates the point with the following example, taken from Thompson Clarke:

> Suppose a scientist is experimenting with soporifics, himself the guinea-pig. He is in a small room. He keeps careful records. Experiment No. 1: 1.00 p.m. Taking X dose of drug Z orally . . . 1.15 p.m. Beginning to feel drowsy. I am not focusing on . . . 6.15 p.m. I've been asleep but am wide awake now, rested and feeling normal. *I know*, of course, *that I am not now dreaming*, but I remember, while asleep, actually thinking I was really awake, not dreaming. (Ibid., p. 256)

Stroud goes on:

> The experimenter says he knows he is not dreaming now.
> It would be . . . ludicrous to say that he thereby settles in
> the affirmative the philosophical question whether we can
> ever know that we are not dreaming. . . . [But these]
> remarks are none the worse for not answering philosophi-
> cal questions. They are to be undersood as 'plain', and not
> 'philosophical' remarks. Clarke puts it by saying that the
> knowledge expressed by this experimenter who says he
> knows he is not dreaming is 'plain' knowing. We no more
> expect him to go on to explain how he knows he is not
> dreaming now than we expect a similar explanation to be
> added to a careful report of an experiment in chemistry.
> The question is not deemed relevant to whether the
> person knows. (Ibid., p. 265)

Stroud believes, therefore, that when the experimenter says,
'I know that I am not now dreaming', what he says, as a remark
made within ordinary life, is perfectly legitimate and *true*. The
possibility that he might even now be dreaming and believe
quite wrongly that he is awake, as he did during the course of
the experiment, is, in the context, irrelevant to both the
legitimacy and the truth of his knowledge claim; it is simply a
wild and outrageous suggestion that does not even have to be
considered. In ordinary life we can legitimately and truly say
that we know that we are not dreaming. On the other hand,
Stroud believes that this true ordinary assertion quite clearly
fails to answer the philosophical problem that Descartes raises
in the *First Meditation*, when he asks whether he can know that
he is seated by the fire in his dressing gown and not lying asleep
dreaming in bed. Moreover, in the philosophical context in
which Descartes raises this question, it does seem quite legitimate to object that any ground that Descartes may offer for
the claim to know that he is not dreaming may itself be merely
the result of a dream; in a philosophical context, the objective
understanding of our position that we seek allows the dream-
possibility perpetually to recur and undermine any ground that
might be offered for ruling it out. What Descartes discovers,

therefore, is that when his enquiry is not governed by the restrictions that operate on ordinary practice, he cannot claim to know that he is not now dreaming, and hence cannot claim to know any external fact whatever.

Stroud regards these differences between the experimenter's position and that of Descartes as revealing that the two are actually using the words 'I know that I am not now dreaming' in completely different ways. The meaning of the experimenter's words is held to be a function of their normal usage within everyday contexts, and they are held to be assessed for truth or falsity by our ordinary, empirical methods for the confirmation or disconfirmation of hypotheses. The meaning of Descartes's words, by contrast, is held to be dependent on the conception of objectivity already introduced. When we say, in the philo-sophical mode, 'I am not now dreaming' or 'I know that I am not now dreaming', we are asserting something that either obtains or not independently of whether anyone ever does, or even can, know that it obtains. Stroud writes:

> In seeming to find the dream-possibility intelligible even though no one could ever know things about the world, I am no doubt revealing my continued attachment to what in Chapter Two I called the traditional conception of objectivity or of how it is possible for us to think about the objective world. I think it is very difficult to free oneself from that conception or to see how or why it cannot be correct. On that view, whether I am dreaming or not is simply a question of which state I am in. What matters is only whether the conditions under which it would be true that I am dreaming are fulfilled. (Ibid., p. 273)

Stroud's view, then, is that there are two distinct realms of discourse, both of which provide (or appear to provide) legitimate and intelligible contexts of enquiry, and which are independent of one another to the extent both of the meaning and the truth-values that they assign to the very same words. The relation between these two realms of discourse appears to be this. The philosophical enquiry is concerned with the question whether our knowledge claims can survive the lifting of the restriction to our normal human perspective, which governs our ordinary knowledge claims, and succeed as claims addressed to reality 'objectively conceived'. For Stroud, the fundamental question raised by scepticism is whether knowledge claims are true only if they are understood empirically, as confined claims concerning the realm of human experience (Stroud suggests that this would be a version of idealism), or whether they can still be sustained understood as unrestricted claims concerning what is objectively the case. He seems to believe that the former view (idealism) is really no better than scepticism. He also seems to think that the sceptic has at least succeeded in showing that *if* knowledge claims, understood in the way the philosopher understands them, are intelligible, *then* they cannot be sustained. The problem, therfore, is chiefly one of showing how we can repudiate the conception of objectivity which appears to make philosophical scepticism inevitable, without either courting a form of idealism that is, in a sense, as pessimistic regarding the possibility of objective knowledge as scepticism itself, or seeming to deny something that we do all understand perfectly well. His book ends with a question:

> The challenge is to reveal the incoherence of the traditional conception, and perhaps even to supply an alternative [account of objectivity that] we can understand, without falling once again into a form of idealism that conflicts with what we already know about the independence of the world or denies the intelligibility of the kind of objectivity we already make very good sense of.
>
> Can that be done? Can any account satisfy us? We will not have got to the bottom of scepticism until we have answers to these questions. (Ibid., p. 274)

On Stroud's weak version of the doctrine of the insulation of ordinary practice from the conclusions of philosophical scepticism, our ordinary knowledge claims and those of the philosopher were to be understood as objective in precisely the same sense. However, it was held that in ordinary life we are concerned not with the truth of these objective claims but with the expediency of making and acting on them. On the strong version of the doctrine, our ordinary knowledge claims are alleged to possess a meaning such that they may actually be true even though knowledge claims made in a philosophical context, in what appear to be the very same words, are false. It clearly follows from this that Stroud must believe one of the following two things about the import of our ordinary claims. Either they are not to be understood as objective claims at all, but as subjective claims about how things appear. Or they are to be understood as objective claims only in some restricted ('empirical') sense of objective, while claims made in a philosophical context are objective in some entirely unrestricted ('transcendental') sense. Only if our ordinary claims are understood in one of these two ways can their truth possibly be independent of the truth of the philosophical assertion that we can never know objectively whether or not we are dreaming. The compatibility between scepticsm and ordinary practice must be achieved either by depriving all our ordinary claims of objective import, or by doubling up on the concept of objectivity and insisting that our ordinary notion is a confined one, while the one philosophers employ is pure or unrestricted.

It seems to me that it is certainly impossible to feel content with the first method for achieving compatibility between the truth of our ordinary knowledge claims and the truth of the sceptic's conclusion. For it seems to be quite clearly part of our ordinary conception that what we are claiming, in claiming to know something, is something such that its being the case is independent of anyone's knowing it to be the case. The independence of truth from the results of human enquiry is an essential part of our common-sense outlook. Not only that but Stroud seems to concede as much when he initially insists that the conception of objectivity that he is trying to express consists of 'the merest platitudes'. Thus, when he originally introduces the notion as follows:

> In seeking knowledge we are trying to find out what is true, to ascertain how the world is in this or that respect . . . What we want to find out . . . is what is true, what the objective facts of the matter are. And what we

aspire to and eventually claim to know is the objective truth or falsity of [a given proposition] . . . What we aspire to and eventually claim to know is something that holds quite independently of our knowing it or of our being in a position reasonably to assert it. (Ibid., p. 78)

I take it that he intends to attribute this view to us as part of our ordinary understanding of what we are about in seeking and claiming knowledge of reality. It seems, therefore, that the first method for achieving compatibility cannot be what is in question and that Stroud must have in mind some version of the second. That is, he must hold that the truth of our ordinary claims is compatible with the truth of the sceptical conclusion, in virtue of the fact that the philosopher employs a concept of objectivity that out-reaches the conception expressed above, and such that the truth of claims that are objective in the above sense is compatible with the falsity of knowledge claims that are objective in this further sense.

Stroud is never fully explicit about just how we are to understand our ordinary claim 'I know that I am not now dreaming' in such a way as to leave its truth compatible with the truth of the sceptic's assertion 'We can never know whether we are not merely dreaming', and I do not think it ever becomes clear just what he has in mind. Yet it does seem to me entirely plain that any intelligible conception of objectivity will be one such that we would want to say that our ordinary knowledge claims are objective in that very sense. Certainly, Stroud's way of expressing what is at issue when the philosopher asks 'Do I know that I am not now dreaming?', could quite properly be taken to characterize our ordinary understanding of the question. Thus, when he says that the philosopher means the question in such a way that 'whether I am dreaming or not is simply a question of which state I am in. What matters is only whether the conditions under which it would be true that I am dreaming are fulfilled', this seems to apply equally to what we should say we mean by that question in eveyday life. Moreover, it seems clear that the only way to deny that it does so is to insist after all on some explicitly subjective content for our ordinary question. And in that case, the second alternative would simply have led straight back to the first. What seems impossible is to hold *both* that when I claim, in ordinary life, to know that I am not now dreaming, I am claiming to know that the truth-conditions of the sentence 'I am not now dreaming' are currently fulfilled, *and* that the truth of my claim is compatible with its all along being the case that I am dreaming, or with my not really knowing that I am not.

My suggestion is, therefore, that Stroud's interpretation of the relationship between philosophy and ordinary practice cannot avoid an implausible claim concerning the content of our ordinary knowledge claims. It is inevitable that any version of the insulation doctrine must involve some sort of idealist qualification of the content of our ordinary knowledge claims, and this is simply at odds with our own robust conception of what we are doing in claiming knowledge of the world. When I claim to know that I am not now dreaming, or that there are kangaroos in Australia, or that there are nine planets, or that dinosaurs are now extinct, then I am making claims concerning an independent reality. The truth of what I understand myself to be asserting is simply not compatible with the possibility that there are ('objectively') no such things as dinosaurs or planets or kangaroos, or with my not knowing ('objectively') that there are. The clash between our ordinary outlook and that of the philosophical sceptic cannot, without an entirely unconvincing idealist conception of the meaning of our ordinary assertions, be made to disappear.

Stroud's account of the relationship between philosophical scepticism and our ordinary knowledge claims seems unsatisfactory for another reason too. It does not do justice to the fact, remarked in chapter 1, that the construction of the sceptic's argument does not appear to involve any implicit revision, or beefing up, of what is being claimed when we affirm knowledge of the world. The philosopher's understanding of what a claim to knowledge involves appears to remain exactly our ordinary one. What is special about the philosopher's enquiry is that, contemplating human knowledge as a whole, he becomes aware of the mass of unquestioned judgements that form our normal starting point, and raises the question whether our implicit claim to know that these judgements are true can be justified.

In looking critically at our system of judgements, the philosopher appears to do no more than operate with our ordinary concept of knowledge and the conception of objectivity and justification that it already embodies. He is drawing our attention not to the subjectivity of our ordinary knowledge claims but to the presumptuousness of our ordinary conviction that we are in possession of justifications that can sustain claims to know how things stand in objective reality. What the sceptical argument reveals is not the idealist content of our ordinary claims, but that our ordinary practice of justifying claims to know about the world is apparently not well-grounded. It seems to follow from this that the point of focus in our search for a resolution of the sceptical problematic should not be the concept of objectivity at all, but the question whether there is a non-sceptical interpretation of the fact that the judgements that form the framework of our practice cannot be justified.

Stroud's ground for the strong version of the insulation doctrine is the fact that we cannot but regard our ordinary knowledge claims as true, but that this does not in itself appear to be a satisfactory refutation of the sceptic. I think that both of these observations are quite correct. However, they do not on their own appear sufficient to motivate Stroud's attempt to cut loose our ordinary assertions from the contemplative assessment of our epistemic position. Although Stroud clearly believes that we cannot be content with a sceptical verdict in philosophy, he attempts to reduce the tension surrounding the problem, by developing a doctrine that would create a sort of *modus vivendi* between common sense and the philosophical sceptic. I have tried to argue that neither the weak nor the strong version of this doctrine is satisfactory. I believe that we must accept the tension: we cannot put off our conviction concerning a system of judgements that the sceptic has shown we cannot ultimately justify. The *prima facie* result of the sceptic's argument is to show that our conviction is dogmatic. It is for precisely this reason that the conviction by itself cannot supply a philosophically satisfactory refutation of the sceptic. However, the powerlessness of the sceptic's argument over our common-sense conviction makes it equally impossible to rest content with the sceptical assessment of ordinary practice. We have, therefore, no choice but to strive for a position that allows us both to preserve our common-sense outlook and to show why it is not dogmatic. We must come to see why ordinary practice is not presumptuous, despite the lack of justification at the limit. We have, therefore, no need of Stroud's ploy to undermine the hasty dismissal. The philosophical unsatisfactoriness of the hasty dismissal is already fully apparent: It does not supply the non-sceptical interpretation of the lack of justification for the judgements of the frame that we require.

3

Moore's Defence of Common Sense

In a famous paper, 'Proof of an External World', G. E. Moore appears to take up the challenge to defend unqualified versions of our ordinary knowledge claims against the attacks of philosophers. Moore spends a good deal of time and effort in making it clear that what he hopes to establish in his defence – that is, that there are, and that we know that there are, external objects – must be understood objectively, as free from any idealist or subjectivist qualification. Put very generally, Moore intends to establish that we stand in an objective relation of knowledge to an objective or independent reality. That is, he intends to prove precisely what the sceptic (and the idealist) deny. Yet when it comes, the proof turns out to be very perplexing.

Moore writes 'I can prove now, for instance, that two human hands exist. How? By holding up my two hands and saying, as I make a certain gesture with the right, "Here is one hand", and adding as I make a certain gesture with the left, "and here is another"' ('Proof of an External World', pp. 145–6). He goes on:

> But did I prove just now that two human hands were then in existence? I do want to insist that I did; that the proof which I gave was a perfectly rigorous one; and that it is impossible to give a better or more rigorous proof of anything whatever. Of course, it would not have been a

proof unless three conditions were satisfied; namely, (1) unless the premiss which I adduced as proof of the conclusion was different from the conclusion I adduced it to prove; (2) unless the premiss I adduced was something which I *know* to be the case and not merely something which I believed but which was by no means certain, or something which, though in fact true, I did not know it to be so; and (3) unless the conclusion really did follow from the premisses. But all these three conditions were in fact satisfied by my proof. (Ibid., p. 146)

Expanding on condition (2) in the above paragraph, Moore writes:

I certainly did at the moment *know* that which I expressed by the combinatiion of certain gestures with saying the words 'Here is one hand and here is another'. I *knew* that there was one hand in the place indicated by combining a certain gesture with my first utterance of 'here' and that there was another in the different place indicated by combining a certain gesture with my second utterance of 'here'. How absurd it would be to suggest that I did not know it, but only believed it, and that perhaps it was not the case! You might as well suggest that I do not know that I am standing up and talking – that perhaps after all I am not, and that it is not quite certain that I am. (Ibid., p. 146)

What is perplexing about Moore's proof, clearly, is that while he claims to be proving what sceptical philosophers have denied – that there are, and that we know that there are, external objects – his proof depends on premises which simply assert particular instances of the very thing that is in doubt. The philosopher's worry is that we are never in a position to claim knowledge of the external world. Moore asserts that he is in a position to give 'a large number of different proofs' of the existence of external objects, any one of which would put him in a position to claim to know external facts. But instead of going on to provide what the sceptic would consider a genuine justification for a particular claim to know some external fact, or even some more general reply to the sceptical objection that all our justifications for claims to know external facts rest on an unproved assumption, Moore simply asserts two particular claims as premises and then derives a general conclusion from them. He then goes on to insist that it would be 'absurd' to suggest that he did not really know what he had claimed in his premises. Yet this is, of course, precisely what the sceptical philosopher does suggest, and with apparently very good reason. Thus, Moore's reply to the sceptic depends on claims to know at least two external facts, which do not so much as address themselves to the objections that the sceptic regards as fatal to our ability to enter or sustain such claims. Moore's alleged reply to the 'scandal' of scepticism seems to beg the question so blatantly that it becomes a matter of real puzzlement how Moore could possible have supposed himself to be offering a serious philosophical challenge to the sceptic at all. One begins to feel that either Moore must have misunderstood the sceptic, or we must be misunderstanding Moore.

Barry Stroud has argued for one particular version of the first hypothesis. The glaring unsatisfactoriness of Moore's proof arises, he claims, because Moore fundamentally misunderstands the nature of the sceptic's question. Stroud's conception of the relationship between scepticism and ordinary practice, discussed in the previous chapter, is vital to his interpretation of Moore and to his diagnosis of the particular way in which his proof fails to engage with the issues raised by philosophical scepticism. Having rejected Stroud's view of the relationship between scepticism and common sense, I want now to consider, and ultimately reject, his interpretation of Moore. I want also to offer an alternative account both of what Moore is doing in his proof and of what makes the proof philosophically unsatisfactory.

Stroud believes that our natural reaction to Moore's proof is much the same as our reaction to the remarks of the experimenter on soporifics, quoted in chapter 2, p. 31 above. We feel, on the one hand, that when Moore says 'I know that this is a hand', what he says is perfectly legitimate and even true, and on the other, that it does not thereby succeed in answering the philosophical question of our knowledge of external facts. Stroud suggests that the philosophical importance of Moore's proof lies in the fact that it forces us to consider how this could possibly be the case:

> I think that what Moore says, understood as he means it, is perfectly acceptable. If it nevertheless seems completely irrelevant to the philosophical questions and does not refute the paradoxical conclusions philosophers reach, that is a very important fact about these philosophical questions and conclusions. It will now need to be explained more carefully why the philosophical questions are not answered if everything Moore says is correct. That would focus attention on what I think is the right issue: precisely how the questions and assertions of the traditional philosopher are related to the questions and assertions we express in the very same words every day without managing to raise or answer philosophical questions. (*The Significance of Philosophical Scepticism*, p. 120)

The conclusion of Stroud's enquiry into what he thinks is 'the right issue' is, as we have seen, that there is a 'distinction between two different ways of speaking, or two different ways of taking the same words'. There is the empirical or plain employment of words in everyday life, where the meaning (or ground for asserting) is governed by a general restriction to the perspective of human beings who must decide and act; and there is the philosophical employment of words, where the meaning (or ground for asserting) is allegedly governed by the philosophical conception of objectivity that Stroud attempts to introduce. Stroud suggests that we can explain our reaction to Moore's proof if we see it as constructed within, and addressed purely to questions that belong to, the empirical realm of discourse. According to Stroud, Moore refuses, or is unable, to 'take his own or anyone else's words in . . . (an) "external" or "philosophical" way' (ibid., p. 119); Moore 'resists, or more probably does not even feel the pressure towards the philosophical project as it is understood by the philosophers he discusses' (ibid., p. 119). Moore's assertions can strike us as true because we recognize them for the ordinary, everyday assertions that they are. At the same time, they can strike us as failing to answer any philisophical question because we understand that the truth (assertability) of these ordinary assertions is entirely insulated from the questions and conclusions that arise within the realm of philosophical enquiry. On Stroud's doctrine of the insulation of ordinary practice from philosophy, what Moore says may be (and is) true, but at the same time it says nothing that is relevant to establishing or refuting any philosophical doctrine whatsoever.

Given his view of the relationship between philosophical and everyday assertions, Stroud is suggesting that Moore responds to the sceptic in the way that he does because he wrongly interprets the sceptic's question as belonging to the empirical realm of discourse. Thus, Moore is held to be somehow incapable of hearing the questions 'Are there any external objects?', or 'Do we know any external facts?', in the way that the philosophical sceptic intends them. The sceptic is asking an external question, a question that concerns reality, and our relation to it, 'objectively conceived', independently of the perspective that human beings occupy. But Moore, Stroud suggests, takes the sceptic's question to be one that is both asked and answerable within the human perspective of common sense. According to Stroud, Moore hears the sceptic's question as we would, in an ordinary practical context, hear the question 'Are there any major rivers in North Africa?', or 'Does anyone know whether there are any major rivers in North Africa?'. Stroud believes, of course, that this is a perfectly legitimate way to take the words 'Are there any external objects?', or 'Do we know any external facts?', and that understood this way, Moore gives the correct answer to the questions they express. But the point is that this is not how the philosopher is using these words; the philosophical question that he expresses cannot be answered by producing examples of knowledge claims that are sustainable within an ordinary human perspective, for that perspective is being transcended in a superior or more absolute conception of objectivity. Thus, Stroud's doctrine of insulation allows him to offer a clear diagnosis of how on earth Moore could have thought that the sceptic's question *could* be answered by producing instances of knowledge claims that would be accepted as true within our ordinary practice.

Stroud's interpretation of Moore's proof is intended to have two principal effects. On the one hand, it is intended to make Moore's response to the questions 'Are there external objects?', 'Do we know external facts?', entirely comprehensible, and even quite correct. On the other, it is intended to show that both these questions, as understood by Moore, and Moore's response to them, are wholly disengaged from the philosophical conclusion of the sceptic. What philosophical relevance Moore's proof does have lies, for Stroud, purely in its tendency to focus the mind on the 'right issue', that is, the relation between philosophical assertions and those made within everyday life. Our immediate recognition that Moore's proof fails to answer the sceptic leads on, Stroud believes, to a significant philosophical discovery about the relation between the philosopher's question and one that might be asked and answered within our ordinary practice; that is, it leads straight to Stroud's insulation doctrine.

It is clear from Moore's own writings that Moore does not share Stroud's doctrine of the insulation of our ordinary knowledge claims from the conclusions of the philosophical sceptic. Moore quite clearly intends that his claim, 'I know that here is one hand and here is another', and the conclusion he basis on it, should be taken in as robust a sense as possible; he is quite explicit that he intends to claim something that is completely unqualified and as objective as can be. Thus, Moore believes that whatever sense the philosophical sceptic's conclusion has, it must be a sense such that its truth is in outright conflict with the truth of the conclusion of his proof. I am, of course, in complete agreement with Moore on this point. I believe not only that our ordinary claims are 'fully objective', but also that the correct way to construe the sceptic's argument is to see it as purporting to show that we lack proper justifications for our ordinary knowledge claims, and that therefore these claims are false and ought not to be made. Moreover, I believe that there is a perfectly satisfactory interpretation of what Moore is doing in his proof that preserves this intuition of an outright conflict between the philosophical assessment of our ordinary practice and our engaged assessment of it. Indeed, I believe it is only if we see the sceptic's conclusion as at odds with our ordinary judgements and claims to knowledge that we can see why Moore takes himself, on the one hand, to establish, by means of his proof, something that is incompatible with the truth of what the sceptic says, and on the other, to have a reply to the sceptic of which we cannot but recognize the power. For it must be admitted, Moore believes, that we do all feel absolutely convinced that Moore does indeed *know* the propositions that form the premises of his proof and the conclusion that he basis on them. Thus, what I want to argue is that Moore is using the fact that scepticism is simply beyond belief, and the fact that it is in conflict with what we are all absolutely convinced of, in an attempt to rout the sceptic. Moore is, if you like, offerring us a version of the sort of 'hasty dismissal' that Stroud's doctrine of insulation is intended to undercut.

On this interpretation of Moore's proof, it is no longer a matter of puzzlement how Moore could have missed the fact that his rebuttal of scepticism does not provide the justifications that the sceptic seeks but simply insists dogmatically on the opposite of what the sceptic claims. For of course Moore does not miss this at all. He is perfectly well aware that his proof begs the question against the sceptic. Thus, in an earlier paper, he writes:

> It seems to me that such a position [that one is incapable of knowing external facts] must, in a certain sense, be quite incapable of disproof. So much must be granted to any sceptic who feels inclined to hold it. Any valid argument which can be brought against it must be of the nature of a *petitio principii*: it must beg the question at issue. How is the sceptic to prove to himself that he does know any external facts? He can only do it by bringing forward some instance of an external fact, which he does know; and, in assuming that he does know this one, he is, of course, begging the question at issue. It is therefore quite impossible for anyone to prove, in one strict sense of the term, that he does know external facts. I can only prove that I do, by assuming that in some particular instance, I actually do know one. That is to say, the so-called proof must assume

the very thing which it pretends to prove. The only proof that we do know external facts lies in the simple fact that we do know them. And the sceptic can with perfect internal consistency deny that he does know any. ('Hume's Philosophy', p. 160)

It is clear, therefore, that Moore believes that *any* rejection of scepticism must appear, from the sceptic's point of view, to beg the question at issue; it must assume knowledge of some external fact. Scepticism and the question-begging assertion of common sense provide, for Moore, the only two available positions. Moore believes that it simply is not possible to *defend* common sense against the sceptic, in the sense of proving in a non-question-begging way that one does know some external fact. However, given that this is our position, it seems entirely clear to him that it could never be more reasonable to embrace a doctrine that we are all completely convinced is false than to reaffirm the judgements and knowledge claims that we are all completely convinced are true. Given the conflict between scepticism and common sense, and given our inability to feel our faith in our common-sense assertions even so much as shaken by the sceptic's argument, the only reasonable response must be to reject scepticism and reaffirm our common-sense view. Moore sums up the point as follows:

There is no reason why we should not . . . make our philosophical opinions agree with what we necessarily believe at other times. There is no reason why I should not confidently assert that I really do *know* some external facts, although I cannot prove the assertion except by simply assuming that I do. I am, in fact, as certain of this as of anything, and as reasonably certain of it. (Ibid., p. 163)

Moore repeats these points at the end of the paper 'Proof of an External World' when he acknowledges that many philosophers will feel dissatisfied with his proof, on the ground that he does not prove what he claims to know in the premises of his proof. Again, he affirms his conviction that the proofs these philosophers seek cannot be given. And again, it is clear that he does not think that the absence of proof, in this sense, could ever make it reasonable for him to give up what he is firmly convinced of, namely that he does really know the propositions he expresses with the words, 'Here is one hand, and here is another'. He writes:

> I can make an approach to explaining what [many philosophers] want by saying that if I had proved the propositions which I used as *premises* in my . . . (proof) then they would perhaps admit that I had proved the existence of external things, but in the absence of such a proof (which, of course, I have neither given nor attempted to give), they will say that I have not given what they mean by a proof of the existence of external things. In other words, they want a proof of what I assert *now,* when I hold up my hands and say 'Here's one hand and here's another' . . . Of course, what they really want is not merely a proof of [this] proposition, but something like a general statement as to how *any* proposition of this sort may be proved. This, of course, I haven't given, and I do not believe it can be given: if this is what is meant by a proof of external things, I do not believe that any proof of external things is possible. (Ibid., p. 149)

He goes on:

> I can know things which I cannot prove; and among the things which I certainly did know, even if (as I think) I could not prove them, were the premises of my two proofs. I should say, therefore, that those, if any, who are dissatisfied with these proofs merely on the ground that I did not know their premises, have no good reason for their dissatisfaction. (Ibid., p. 150)

What I am suggesting, therefore, is that Moore's response to the sceptic is only properly understood in the light of his acceptance, on the one hand, of the two assumptions that I have taken as the frame for my discussion of scepticism, namely that it is both unanswerable and unliveable, and on the other, of the view, which I also share, that the sceptic's conclusion is in outright conflict with our common-sense conviction that we do really know a mass of external facts. Given the conflict, and given the utter powerlessness of the sceptic's argument to *persuade* us of the doubtfulness of our ordinary world view, Moore believes that the only reasonable response must be to reject the sceptical conclusion; that is to say, he believes it would be completely unreasonable to espouse a philosophical doctrine that we are, at all other times, convinced is false. Even though it is true that the sceptic's conclusion comes at the end of a *prima facie* good argument, the argument should not be allowed to influence our philosophical views, for, on the other side, our much more powerful conviction that we do know an enormous number of external facts makes the espousal of philosophical scepticism unreasonable and absurd. The only reasonable attitude in philosophy is one that is in harmony with what we necessarily believe at all other times.

It seems to me, therefore, that Moore's response to scepticism is entirely intelligible, provided we allow that scepticism and common sense are in outright conflict with one another. For then it is possible to understand how Moore could regard our inability to live sceptical doubt, or to believe the sceptical conclusion, as a reason for rejecting scepticism altogether. If, as Stroud tries to argue, the truth of all our ordinary assertions were entirely compatible with the truth of the sceptic's conclusion, then, of course, the inescapability of our common-sense attitudes could not motivate any particular response to the sceptic. Thus, it is at bottom Stroud's own view of the relation between scepticism and our ordinary knowledge claims that makes it impossible for him to understand how Moore could regard such a brazenly question-begging insistence that we do know external facts as philosophically interesting, or as relevant to the problem raised by the sceptic. I am suggesting that, if one goes along with Moore, and sees the sceptic's conclusion as in conflict with common sense, then Moore's response can be seen as an argument from the complete inability of scepticism to bring conviction to its total intellectual bankruptcy, and as such it ceases altogether to be a matter for puzzlement.

I have argued that Moore's proof is comprehensible as a response to the philosophical sceptic. The question whether it constitutes a philosophically satisfactory response is, of course, another matter. It is clear that, on the current interpretation, there is an entirely explicit element of dogmatism in Moore's proof. I have argued that this dogmatic element does not make Moore's putting forward the proof as a reply to the sceptic a matter for puzzlement; it is perfectly possible to understand why Moore believed that the dogmatic rejection of scepticism is the only philosophically reasonable response to make: the only alternative (acceptance of scepticism) is, given our natural conviction that it is false, entirely *un*reasonable. However, I believe that one must in the end accept that this dogmatic element renders Moore's reply philosophically *un*satisfactory. It is not, of course, that I believe that the dogmatism can be avoided by providing the missing proofs for the premises of Moore's argument, for I share Moore's conviction that the sceptic is, in this sense, unanswerable. But I also think that there are clear objections to the view that, in the absence of these justifications, we can simply insist that we do really know.

First of all, it seems to me that Moore's dogmatism is, by the principles of the practice he means to defend, an unacceptable response to a demonstration that one lacks the requisite justification to sustain a knowledge claim. It is impossible to use our conviction that the sceptic's conclusion is false as a legitimate ground for dismissing scepticism, for it is clearly part of our ordinary grasp of the concept of knowledge that personal conviction is never sufficient to warrant the affirmation of a knowledge claim exposed as doubtful. Possessing an adequate justification for believing a given proposition, p, is part of our normal ground for asserting a claim to know p. If the sceptic is correct that all our justifications for beliefs concerning external facts rest on the unproved assumption (that experience is a reliable guide to the nature of reality), then he has shown that we never possess a justification adequate to sustain a knowledge claim concerning the external world. What the sceptic shows, in other words, is that, by the principles that ordinarily govern the entering of a knowledge claim, we cannot claim to know any external fact. It is, therefore, contrary to our ordinary ways of proceeding to insist, in the face of the sceptic's objection, that one is entirely warranted in claiming that one is not merely convinced but that one really does *know* that the proposition expressed by 'Here is one hand and here is another' is true.

Thus, the trouble with Moore's (or with any) version of the 'hasty dismissal' of the sceptic's conclusion is that it is, from the point of view of common sense itself, unacceptable: knowledge claims cannot be warranted or established as correct merely by the insistence that one really does know. The ambivalence that we feel concerning Moore's proof arises, I believe, precisely because it make us feel the tension between the unliveability and the unanswerability of scepticism. On the one hand, we cannot but recognize that we are indeed convinced that Moore does know what he claims to know in the premises of his proof; on the other, we cannot but feel that he has no right to say he knows it. We are, therefore, brought face to face with the profound discomfort of a state of affairs in which we cannot answer the sceptic but no more can we believe him. Having been led to make a claim to know a representative judgement of the frame, and having been made to acknowledge the difficulty of justifying it, we cannot then escape the sense that the *legitimate* reaffirmation of these judgements, and of the knowledge claims we base on them, awaits the provision of a justification for the unproved assumption that appears to underlie our apparent conviction that we *know* these framework judgements. Given that we, like Moore, accept that this justification cannot be provided, we feel that it is impossible to go back to affirming our judgements and knowledge claims, without saying anything more about it, as if it were an entirely normal procedure in the face of unanswerable objections to a claim to know. Our immediate sense of the unsatisfactoriness of Moore's proof, even given that we are convinced that he does really know what he claims to know, serves to bring out with great clarity that common sense cannot on its own provide a philosophically satisfactory reply to the sceptic.

The idea that in order for a defence of common sense to be philosophically satisfactory something more must be said brings us to the second source of unsatisfactoriness in Moore's proof. By ignoring the need to resolve the tension between the unliveability and the unanswerability of scepticism, Moore abandons all chance of a real resolution of the problem. Thus, aside from going against our ordinary understanding of the words 'I know', Moore's proof is unsatisfactory in so far as it does not *earn* our commitment to common sense, by means of a philosophical understanding of *why* the impossibility of grounding our framework judgements does not constitute a threat to, or demonstrate a failure of, our ordinary practice. A genuine resolution of the riddle of scepticism must allow us to see why our inability to justify the judgements that represent our normal starting point is not a lack of any thing essential. If we accept that we cannot answer the sceptic, or provide the justifications he believes are required, then the way to retrieve our common-sense conviction must be to provide an understanding of the workings of ordinary practice on which our rationally ungrounded conviction no longer appears to have the status of unwarranted presumption. The unsatisfactoriness of digging in one's heels, aside from being against the principles of ordinary practice, is that it leaves us, as far as the philosophical understanding of the significance of the problem of scepticism is concerned, exactly where we were at the outset.

In the end, then, I want to suggest that Moore's defence of common sense, although perfectly intelligible, is not philosophically satisfactory. I am, therefore, in agreement with Stroud that something essential to the resolution of the problem of scepticism is missing from Moore's reply. However, as I see it the lack does not arise because Moore's proof belongs to a realm of discourse entirely disjointed from that in which philosophical illumination of our epistemic position is sought. Rather, it is simply that, while the conclusion of Moore's proof is at once one we are, in normal circumstances, entirely convinced of, and one that is in outright conflict with the conclusion of the philosophical sceptic, it does not provide any understanding of why our normal conviction is not a piece of unacceptable dogmatism. Thus, we can understand the philosophical failure of Moore's proof simply by acknowledging that any satisfactory rebuttal of the sceptic must not ignore but resolve the tension between the fact that we cannot doubt, and the fact that we cannot justify, our ordinary world view. As far as we are concerned the main advantage of contemplating Moore's proof is not that it uncovers two distinct ways of employing words but that it makes clear the need to understand *why* the sceptic's argument does not show that our common-sense conviction is out of place, and *why* that conviction does not constitute a dogmatic assertion of assumptions held without the requisite justification.

Although I have argued against Stroud's view that there is a special realm of philosophical discourse, in which the philosopher uses our words but with a special sense or import, it now seems clear that I am committed to the existence of something called 'philosophical understanding'. Thus, the above objection to Moore's proof makes it clear that I do believe that there is a task for philosophy to perform and that that task cannot be accomplished by the bare assertion of our common-sense outlook. There is something needed in addition to common sense; some sort of understanding *of* common sense, that allows us to see, not only how it functions, but why we can 'feel content' with it, why its functioning is not properly subject to the objections of the sceptic. At the moment, just what would satisfy this need for an understanding of ourselves and our practice is obscure, but I think that Moore's proof has at least made it clear that there *is* something that we need, and that 'entrenched common-sensism' does not supply it.

4

On the Significance of What We Would Ordinarily Doubt

It is an important part of Moore's response to the sceptic that he believes that our philosophical views should not be at odds with what we necessarily believe at other times. J. L. Austin has a similar conviction that philosophy becomes absurd whenever it finds itself in conflict with common sense. It is, indeed, this concern to develop a philosophy that is at once in no way at odds with, and in no sense a qualification of, our ordinary robust and optimistic view about our capacity to know about the world, that I have taken as the common characteristic of the philosophers I am discussing. However, Austin's response to the traditional epistemologist appears *prima facie* to avoid Moore's dogmatism, and to provide the sort of understanding I have suggested is to be hoped for from a philosophically satisfactory reply to the sceptic. That is to say, Austin does appear to offer an account of why the sceptic's discovery of a lack of justification underlying the entire structure of our ordinary knowledge claims is spurious or merely apparent: he tries to show why the justification that the sceptic seeks is not actually requisite in order for our ordinary knowledge claims to be quite correctly sustained.

Austin's attitude towards the sceptic is much the same as his attitude towards the sense-data theorist. The philosophical confusion into which the sceptic is led, with its absurd conclusion that we do not know external facts, is to be seen as the result of the philosopher's having 'not really understood or carefully studied or correctly described' (*Sense and Sensibilia*, p. 3) our use of certain key words, in this case the words 'I know'. His belief seems to be that once we do pay careful attention to how we actually use the words 'I know', and derive a detailed account of what is actually requisite for knowledge, then the sceptic's reasoning will no longer have any power to tempt us into its inevitable trap. The sceptic's argument will have been exposed for what it is: 'a mass of seductive (mainly verbal) fallacies' (ibid., p. 5). Thus, Austin attempts, by careful description of the use of the words 'I know', to reveal that the philosopher's insistence that we can never know any external fact, because we can never know whether or not our experience is merely the result of a dream or is brought about at the instigation of an evil genius, is based on a fundamental misconception of the rules of practice (use) that are constitutive of the meaning of the words 'I know'. Once the employment (meaning) of our words is brought clearly into focus, then we shall see that the sceptic's objection to our ordinary knowledge claims is in fact not a legitimate objection at all.

On the face of it, then, Austin's procedure does appear to offer some understanding *of* common sense, or *of* the workings of ordinary practice, that might earn us the right to continue to affirm all our ordinary knowledge claims. Austin's method offers out the hope of a genuine resolution of the tension between the unanswerability and the unliveability of scepticism, through the demonstration that the intuitions about the meaning (or use) of the words 'I know' on which the crucial stages 4–6 (see p. 6 above) of the sceptic's agrument depends are simply wrong. What we find, according to Austin, is that there is after all no case to answer: the meaning of the words 'I know' is such that we are not required to remove the sort of sceptical counter-possibility that the sceptic constructs in order to sustain a knowledge claim. And this does appear to be one clear way of showing both why the sceptic's attempt to argue that our system of knowledge claims is not well-grounded misfires, and why the judgements that form the framework of our practice are not lacking a sort of justification that they strictly require. The tension between the unliveability and the

unanswerability of scepticism is resolved honourably, by dis-
solving (rather than by resolutely turning one's back on) the
sceptic's agrument. The need to eliminate the sceptical hypotheses that are used to undermine a representative knowledge
claim concerning a judgement of the frame is shown to be
merely apparent, for it depends on a misunderstanding or
misdescription of our epistemic concepts.

According to Austin, the traditional epistemologist's tendency, first to misunderstand the concept of knowledge, and
then to find himself in the sceptical quagmire, arises because he
neglects the task of accurately describing the circumstances in
which we deem someone to know a given proposition. The
traditional epistemologist attempts to conjure the concept of
knowledge virtually out of thin air, by thinking about a few
poorly described and unrealistic examples. The traditional
epistemologist's intuitions about what is requisite for knowledge simply do not survive once we begin to imagine detailed
cases of concrete claims to know. Austin's criticism of the
traditional epistemologist might, therefore, be summed up in a
slogan of Wittgenstein's: 'Dont't think, but look!' (PI, 66).
Austin himself puts the point as follows: 'words are our tools,
and, as a minimum, we should use clean tools: we should know
what we mean and what we do not, and we must forearm
ourselves against the traps that language sets for us' ('A Plea for
Excuses' pp. 129–30).

Austin's method is to replace the vague and disastrous
intuitions of the traditional epistemologist with precisely arti-
culated observations based on detailed examinations of 'what
we should say when'. His view is that by thus paying attention to
what words we would deem it correct to use in carefully
imagined concrete cases, we are actually clarifying the phenomenon of knowledge itself; we are bringing into much sharper
focus what it is actually to know something. He writes:

> When we examine what we should say when, what words
> we should use in what situations, we are looking . . . not
> *merely* at words . . . but also at the realities we use the
> words to talk about: we are using a sharpened awareness of
> words to sharpen our perception of, though not as the
> final arbiter of, the phenomena. (Ibid., p. 130)

Austin thought that the best name for this method of philosophizing might be 'linguistic phenomenology', with its suggestion that one way to investigate the phenomena is to investigate the language we employ in talking about the phenomena. It is not, as Austin is careful to stress, that the method considers ordinary language to be the 'final arbiter' of what constitute the phenomena. Rather, it is that our employment of language presents the most promising starting point for finding out what the phenomena we talk about are; careful description of how we use words offers out the best hope of achieving a view of language *and* the phenomena on which we will no longer be liable to the shocks of the philosopher's 'seductive (mainly verbal) fallacies'. He makes the point as follows: 'Certainly, then, ordinary language is *not* the last word: in principle it can everywhere be supplemented and improved upon and superseded. Only remember, it *is* the *first* word' (ibid, p. 133).

What, then, does Austin think we discover about what it is to know a given proposition when we make a detailed investigation of the use of the words 'I know' in carefully imagined concrete cases? The case that Austin takes is one of seeing a bird in clear view in a garden and remarking 'That's a goldfinch' ('Other Minds', p. 45). What Austin is interested in is the circumstances or conditions under which we will regard the claim to know what sort of bird the bird in the garden is to be correct. In particular, he hopes, by means of an examination of the conditions under which certain sorts of *objection* may be made to the knowledge claim, to uncover, or bring into sharper focus, what it is to *know* that the bird in the garden is a goldfinch.

The first thing that Austin observes is that whenever we make a claim to know a given proposition, p, we are always liable to be asked the question: How do you know p? The question, 'How do you know?', may be asked 'only out of respectful curiosity, from a genuine desire to learn' (ibid., p. 46). But on the other hand, the question may also be asked 'pointedly', from a suspicion that the speaker does not really know, and cannot sustain his claim. Asked with this second import, the question is a form of *challenge* to the claim to know p; it invites the speaker to satisfy us that he is indeed in a position to know what he has claimed. It is, of course, the conditions governing this second way of asking the question that we are interested in. For clearly, when the traditional epistemologist asks 'How do I know?' of a representative framework judgement – e.g. when Descartes asks, 'How do I know that I am seated by the fire in my dressing gown, and not asleep dreaming in bed?' – he does *not* ask out of respectful curiosity, from a genuine desire to learn, but pointedly, out of a sudden suspicion that he might not *know* at all.

The question 'How do you know?' is to be taken, therefore, as a challenge to the claimant to provide adequate grounds for his claim. Austin now suggests that, having been thus challenged, the claimant must indicate features of the situation that enable him to recognize it as one that is correctly described in the way he has described it. He must 'indicate, or to some extent set out with some degree of precision, those features of the situation which enable [him] to recognize it as one to be described in the way [he] did describe it' (ibid., p. 51). Thus, in the current case, the claimant must say what it is about the bird in the garden that enables him to recognize it as a goldfinch. Austin imagines him replying, 'From its behaviour', or 'By its markings', or 'By its red head', or 'From its eating thistles'.

The next stage is to consider the circumstances under which someone might legitimately object that the grounds that are offered for the claim do not actually sustain it. Here Austin distinguishes two main types of objection. First of all, someone might dispute the grounds that have been offered for the claim: e.g. 'That's not a red head, that's orange', or 'Those aren't thistles'. Second, someone may not dispute the facts given as the ground for the claim but may question whether the grounds provide a sufficient justification of the claim that is based on them. Again, Austin thinks that there are two sorts of case. In the first sort of case the objection tries to establish, not merely that the claimant does not know it is a goldfinch, but that it is not a goldfinch, or rather, the objection tries to establish that the claimant does not know it is a goldfinch because it is not a goldfinch: e.g. 'But goldfinches *don't* have red heads', 'But that's not a goldfinch. From your own description I can recognize it as a goldcrest'. In the second sort of case, the objection attempts to establish merely that the claimant is not in a position to claim to know that the situation is correctly described in the way he suggests: e.g. 'But that's not enough: plenty of other birds have red heads. What you say doesn't prove it. For all you know, it may be a woodpecker.'

It is the conditions governing the final sort of objection – the 'That's-not-enough'-objection – that we are interested in. For again, the sceptic does not challenge Descartes's grounds for his claim to know that he is seated by the fire in his dressing gown (namely, that he *seems* to be awake and to see the fire before him); nor does he try to establish that Descartes is *not* awake and seated by the fire; he merely questions whether the grounds on which Descartes makes his claim to know that he is seated by the fire in his dressing gown are sufficient to support the claim. That is to say, the sceptic's objection is of the form: 'That's not enough: you could be asleep and dreaming, or be deceived by an evil genius, and it still *seem* to you *as if* you were seated by the fire in your dressing gown. For all you know either one of these other possibilities may be the case.'

Austin now makes four observations concerning the 'That's-not-enough'-objection, the following two of which seem to be the crucial ones for understanding how he suggests the traditional epistemologist's intuitions concerning what constitutes genuine knowledge go wrong:

(a) If you say 'That's not enough', then you must have in mind some more or less definite lack. 'To be a goldfinch, besides having a red head it must have the characteristic eye markings'; or 'How do you know it isn't a woodpecker? Woodpeckers have red heads too.' If there is no definite lack which you are at least prepared to specify on being pressed, then it's silly (outrageous) just to go on saying 'That's not enough.'

(b) Enough is enough: it doesn't mean everything. Enough means enough to show that (within reason, and for present intents and purposes) it 'can't' be anything else, there is no room for an alternative, competing, description of it. It does *not* mean, for example, enough to show that it isn't a *stuffed* goldfinch. (Ibid., p. 52)

If we take the step of regarding each of these points as describing conditions that govern the making of an objection of the form 'That's not enough' – i.e. if we view them as restrictions on the conditions under which this form of objection succeeds in undermining a knowledge claim, and as in part constitutive of our concept of knowledge, or of what it is to know something – then it becomes easy enough to see why we are now in a position to resist the fallacies of the sceptic. For it now becomes clear that the sceptic's objection to Descartes's claim to know that he is seated by the fire in his dressing gown is, given these restrictions, illegitimate. First of all, the sceptic's initial objection to the claim is not prompted by any specific feature of the concrete situation, but springs from an entirely general worry that, since he does not know whether experience is a reliable guide to the nature of reality, he cannot be sure that he is ever in a position to know anything about the external world. It is only after he has entered his objection on these purely general grounds that the sceptic even begins to construct alternative competing descriptions of the situation. Second, the alternative descriptions of the situation that the sceptic constructs – 'You may be dreaming' or 'You may be deceived by an evil genius' – are mere long shots, obscure and even outrageous possibilities that no one could reasonably suppose to obtain.

Thus, if we regard Austin's observations as indicating restrictions that govern objections to a use of the words 'I know', or as telling us something significant about the phenomenon of knowing, then it appears to follow that the sceptic has no case. There are no legitimate objections (i.e. objections meeting the conditions Austin describes) to Descartes's claim to know that he is seated by the fire in his dressing gown. It seems, therefore, that a knowledge claim concerning a representative judgement of the frame is capable of being sustained, and that such judgements may therefore quite legitimately ground further claims to know about the world. The sceptic succeeds in making his objection to Descartes look plausible, and in making it seem as if Descartes does not *know* what he claims, only because he first of all seduces us away from a careful investigation of the phenomenon of knowledge and into supposing that *any* objection, made on the basis of *any* sort of counter-possibility, no matter how outrageous or far flung, undermines a claim to know.

Let us suppose that all the observations that Austin makes concerning our employment of the words 'I know' are quite correct. Thus, let us suppose that our ordinary use of the words 'I know', or rather our ordinary practice of objecting to a use of these words, is subject to just the sort of restrictions that Austin describes. Can we now conclude that the sceptic's objection to Descartes's claim to know that he is seated by the fire in his dressing gown is, for the sorts of reason just outlined, inappropriate and out of place, a misuse of our concept of knowledge?

I should perhaps begin by remarking that I do not think there is any hope of saving the sceptic from Austin's criticisms by arguing, à la Stroud, that both the sceptic and Austin give a correct account of two entirely different things. That is, I do not think there is any plausibility in the suggestion that the sceptic correctly presents the conditions under which it is true ('transcendentally' true) that we know something, and that Austin correctly describes the conditions under which it is correct to assert ('empirically' true) that we know something. It seems to me that there is an irreconcilable clash between Austin and the sceptic. The sceptic claims to have uncovered an objection to our entire system of knowledge claims concerning external facts: it rests on judgements which are not well-grounded but depend on the unproved, and unprovable, assumption that experience provides a reliable guide to the nature of reality. If this is correct, then it seems to follow that we cannot be said to know these judgements or any of the judgements that are based on them. Austin claims that careful attention to what is actually constitutive of the phenomenon of knowledge reveals that the sceptic has no legitimate objection to a claim to know a judgement of the frame, and that the objection he enters is based on a form of doubt that is not even relevant to the question whether Descartes knows what he claims. If this is correct, then it would seem to follow that we do know (can sustain a claim to know) the judgements of the frame, and that our system of knowledge is in general well-grounded and secure against doubt. Austin and the sceptic cannot both be right.

The question is: which one is right? Austin, as we have seen, arrives at his account of what is requisite for knowledge via a detailed examination of ordinary practice or 'what we should say when', that is, via a detailed examination of the conditions that govern the entering and criticizing of particular concrete knowledge claims which he imagines being made in a normal context. His observations regarding ordinary practice yield the above objections to the sceptic's alleged undermining of Descartes's claim to know that he is seated by the fire in his dressing gown, only because we have been imagining this as a claim made in an ordinary context, in which our common-sense attitude is in place. It seems, therefore, that the sceptic could reasonably object that by confining his enquiry to what we should say within ordinary practice, Austin necessarily operates in a region where the presumptuous nature of the judgements of the frame is never, and could never be, perceived. The sceptic can then argue that he himself is operating with precisely the concept of knowledge that Austin describes, and that all that is special in his employment of this concept is that it is being used independently of the engaged perspective that makes us blind to the shortcomings of our own epistemic position. Thus, the sceptic may insist that he is not changing the standard of what constitutes an adequate or non-defective ground for a knowledge claim, but simply taking up a contemplative attitude that allows him to perceive that his 'alternative, competing, descriptions' of the origins of experience are not 'outrageous' but perfectly intelligible accounts that must be ruled out if our claim to knowledge is to be sustained. Thus, the contemplative stance is held to reveal a definite defect in the ground of our framework judgements, which we are normally too hasty or too presumptuous to observe. The sceptic might strengthen his case still further by pointing out that practically everyone who is master of the concepts of knowledge and justification, and who follows him in taking up the contemplative stance, is led to admit the extreme cogency of the sceptical reasoning, and to discover the same inadequacies in our epistemic position as the sceptic does.

In his discussion of Austin, Stroud accepts Austin's view that he and the sceptic are in fundamental disagreement over what the conditions for knowledge are. Stroud's view of the sceptic is, as we have already seen, that he is led to make a discovery about the concept of knowledge, that is, that it strictly ('transcendentally') requires a much higher standard of justification (one, namely, that requires that the possibility that we are dreaming be ruled out) than the one we ordinarily operate with. Stroud believes, of course, that the sceptic can argue that he has as much authority for his intuitions as Austin has for his ordinary language observations, and that there is, in that sense, a stand off between the two. However, I am suggesting that the opposition between the sceptic and Austin is not properly captured in this way at all. I want to see the sceptical argument as preserving our epistemic concepts intact and unrevised, so that the disagreement between them is not over what is requisite for knowledge, but lies rather in the entirely different attitudes or stances that they are adopting *vis-à-vis* ordinary practice. The sceptic adopts an attitude that contemplates our ordinary judgements disinterestedly or critically, while Austin's enquiry preserves the engaged, uncritical perspective of common sense itself. From the engaged perspective, the sceptic's doubts concerning a judgement of the frame do indeed look strained and unconvincing, for our ordinary convictions are in place and operational. However, that does not mean that the contemplative critical stance cannot, without any fundamental change in our epistemic concepts, reveal the baselessness of our ordinary conviction and expose it as unwarranted presumption.

It seems, therefore, that Austin's investigation of the conditions requisite for knowledge cannot yield a criticism of the sceptic's understanding of our epistemic concepts at all, for the sceptic can insist that he does not deviate from our ordinary understanding of the concepts of knowledge and justification. The sceptic simply takes his understanding of what is implied by our use of the words 'I know' to be sufficiently clear and secure to be capable of operating independently of any commitment to the correctness of knowledge claims that we would ordinarily regard as immune to objection or beyond all question true. The sceptic employs his established mastery of the concept of knowledge reflectively, independently of our ordinary assessments, in an investigation designed to discover whether our conviction in the well-groundedness of, say, our judgement that this is a hand is actually warranted. Austin clearly believes that such an approach is bound to lead to confusion and that philosophy should (at least) start from a common-sense outlook, and from there investigate, first, the conditons under which we are inclined to make a claim to know something, and second, the conditons under which such a claim is regarded as sustainable or correct. And it is at this point, plainly, that the real disagreement occurs. To start from the assumption that the assessment of judgements that we make from *within* the common-sense outlook is correct is implicitly to deny the possibility of the contemplative stance and the contrary, sceptical, assessment that it yields. Without some philosophical motivation of this methodological assumption that the assessment made from within our practice is correct, and the critical attitude of the sceptic incoherent, Austin's position is no less entrenched, and his rebuttal of scepticism no less dogmatic, than Moore's.

I do not believe that Austin himself ever does perform the real philosophical work of defending the general presupposition of linguistic phenomenology, that is, that our ordinary judgements are for the most part true, and necessarily constitute the phenomena under investigation. The sceptic believes that when we put off our ordinary outlook and adopt a contemplative stance, we discover good reason to doubt the correctness of our ordinary judgements. In the end Austin's dismissal of the sceptic, or rather his commitment to the assessments that we make from our ordinary outlook, depends (like Moore's Proof) on his regarding the sceptic's 'uncovering' of an 'unproved assumption' underlying (and undermining) the entire system as simply the unwarranted doubting of something that we all know to be the case. The dogmatic rebuttal of scepticism is enshrined in Austin's methodological principle that when we ordinarily (i.e. from a common-sense outlook) judge ourselves to know external facts we cannot but, by and large, be right. This view of Austin's method is shared by at least one major expositor of his work. Matts Furberg concedes the essentially Moorean attitudes that lie behind the method as follows:

Like Moore, Austin accepts a large part of the common-sense view as undoubtedly true . . .

As a rule, Austin gives no argument in favour of this commonsense view. He simply assumes that its truth is obvious as soon as it is pointed out: I do sometimes know, without any possibility of doubt, that my wife is very angry indeed . . . The only place where he has defended common sense explicitly and at length is in *Sense and Sensibilia*. But even there he does not argue certain things, presumably because he thinks that any argument for them would rely on more dubious premises that they themselves do. Thus he quotes Ayer as making the 'assumptions' that a stick does not change its shape when placed in water and that it cannot be both crooked and straight; and he remarks that it is both strange and important that Ayer speaks of 'assumptions' here, for it makes it possible for him to 'take seriously the notion of denying at least one of them, which he could hardly do if he had recognised them . . . as the plain and incontestable facts that they are' (*Sense and Sensibilia*, 21n). (*Saying and Meaning*, pp. 7–8)

The point that I am trying to make is that it is in the provision of an understanding of why these things do not constitute 'assumptions', accepted without the requisite justification, that we should look for a philosophically satisfactory rebuttal of scepticism. It is agreed that these things cannot strike us as assumptions from within the engaged perspective of common sense, but that is not enough to constitute a philosophically satisfactory answer. It must be shown, in a philosophical account of the workings of ordinary practice, that this engaged assessment is correct. It is not, therefore, that I wish, in the end, to discard Austin's belief that what knowledge is is revealed by, or manifest in, our ordinary judgements employing the words 'I know'. Rather, the point is that in order to address the sceptical problematic we must provide a philosophical motivation for this view; we must show that 'resting content' with our ordinary judgements is not a case of *presumption* on our part. Thus, it may be conceded that we cannot properly, or practically, enter into any sceptical doubt concerning our ordinary knowledge claims (that we cannot properly treat them as presumptuous), but given the apparently compelling nature of the sceptical discoveries made from the contemplative point of view, we still need to understand why this attitude is not dogmatic. Moore and Austin are both convinced that it is neither inappropriate nor hasty nor dogmatic, even though they cannot show that this is so to the sceptic's satisfaction. But neither Moore nor Austin provides us with an account that explains *why* our attitude is not hasty or dogmatic or presumptuous. The best that they can offer is to say that if each of us thinks about it carefully and without prejudice we too will see that it is not; but this plainly falls short of a philosophically articulate understanding of the fact.

Thus, without intending to denigrate the real philosophical achievements of Austin's phenomenological method, I think that we must conclude that the impresssion that Austin provides the sort of philosophical understanding needed to unravel the riddle of scepticism is in the end illusory. Austin does not reveal the philosophical significance of the fact that we cannot provide justifications for judgements we are normally convinced of but which strike us, from the contemplative stance, as open to question; nor does he provide a non-sceptical understanding of what the absence of these justifications means. Austin's whole philosophical approach begins from a point – that is, the attitude that most of our ordinary judgements are correct – that precludes him from contributing to either of these two tasks. Austin, in effect, dismisses the sceptic immediately, in virtue of the fact that his philosophical method maintains, without establishing our right to maintain, our normal commitment to the correctness of our ordinary judgements. Moore regarded common sense as a reply to the philosophical sceptic's question, and a reply that we all show ourselves to be completely convinced is correct. But Austin's mode of enquiry into the phenomenon of knowledge makes methodological assumptions that make it impossible for him even to hearken to the sceptic's reflections; he has from the beginning, and entirely dogmatically, foreclosed on the possibility of the contemplative stance that is essential to the sceptic's discoveries. Austin's method is to undertake the careful description of common sense and of distinctions that we draw in our ordinary, practical employment of our language; the sort of contemplative enquiry that the sceptic undertakes falls completely outside its brief.

However, it might be objected that there is something that Austin *can* say against the coherence of the sceptic's attitude. As Austin sees it, we are masters of our language, and the idea that we might employ it in systematically false judgements may be rejected outright. The thought has its echo, plainly, in much recent philosophy of language, most notably in Davidson's Principle of Charity (*Inquiries into Truth and Interpretation*, particularly essays 1 and 9). It does at least appear to hint at a motivation for the idea that when the philosopher investigates our ordinary attributions of knowledge, or of responsibility, or of intentional action he is examining instances of the phenomena themselves. And it does at least gesture towards a reason why muddle and confusion are the inevitable consequences of an approach that does not accept that we cannot all be wrong about what we are all talking about. However, it seems to me that the above thought is no more than a hint, and it does not by itself reveal why the attitude that 'we cannot be misusing our words', or 'cannot but be right most of the time', is not merely dogmatic. I suppose that what I am claiming is that the enormous promise of linguistic phenomenology will only be established when the above mentioned hint is upgraded to a clear philosophical account of *why* the apparent absence of justification for a large and vital class of judgements (those that form the frame of our practice) does not render them unwarranted and presumptuous. Thus we need to expand the hint into a complete philosophical understanding of the nature of our participation in ordinary practice, which reveals it as having an undogmatic and non-presumptuous base. Only then will we have fully met the sceptic's challenge to *earn* our conviction in a host of ordinary judgements about the world.

The discussion of Austin's work has brought us, therefore, to the same suggestion as to the sort of philosophical understanding that is needed if we are ever to achieve a satisfactory reply to the sceptic. The element of unsatisfactoriness, as far as answering the sceptic is concerned, enters in because Austin's method does nothing to make his attitude of commitment to common sense look, in the face of the sceptic's reflections, less like the dogmatic assumption of claims that cannot be justified. And this suggests that if we could see our way to providing an account of why the attitude of regarding our ordinary judgements as by and large correct is at once inescapable and undogmatic, then we should be in a position to understand why scepticism misfires as an attempt to show that our common-sense conviction is out of place. The sceptic attempts to put off our ordinary conviction in the correctness of a mass of judgements and knowledge claims concerning external facts, and to estrange himself from our ordinary practice of employing terms; he attempts to become critical of our ordinary modes of employing language and to entertain the possibility that all our judgements and claims concerning external facts are false. Austin's philosophy begins in the methodological assumption that this attitude starts with unintelligibly denying the obvious and leads on to greater and greater outrages against what we all know to be the case. What we want is an account which actually lays bare the precise nature of the unintelligibility and the exact reasons why our inability to justify the mass of common-sense judgements that we do not ordinarily question does not constitute any sort of *lack* or *failure* on our part. Such an account would have earned us common sense as a starting point and would explain why Austin's method is possible.

As our philosophical objective becomes gradually clearer, it begins to emerge even more plainly that the focus of our search for a philosophical resolution of the problem of scepticism is very different from Stroud's. I argued earlier that Stroud is not successful in formulating a position which can both concede a due degree of robustness to our ordinary claims and still allow that, construed objectively, these claims might all be false. I suggested that the meaning of our ordinary claims is such that we cannot tolerate the idea that their truth is compatible with a philosophical assessment of them as false; our ordinary claims are claims to know how things stand in objective reality, and they are simply undermined by the sceptical conclusion. It now seems to me that the link that I have just uncovered between my approach to the problem of scepticism and Austin's linguistic phenomenology suggests a criticism of Stroud's conception of objectivity itself. For Stroud, the idea of the objective world is the idea of something so independent of us and our perspective on it that it might contain none of the things we experience it as containing or believe it to contain. Saddled with this conception of objectivity, it is easy to see why Stroud should believe that it is the origin of the sceptical problem. It seems clear that as soon as we are tempted into construing the objective world as something that transcends whatever can be experienced or conceived from within the perspective of human beings, the sceptic will always be able to demonstrate that we cannot possibly have genuine knowledge of it. Given Stroud's conception of objectivity, scepticism and idealism must inevitably present themselves as the only two equally unsatisfactory alternatives. However, I believe that we are now in a position to see that this outcome is merely a consequence of the fact that Stroud's understanding of the concept of objectivity and of the origins of the sceptical problem is misleading and unhelpful.

On the view of scepticism taken here, the concept of ojectivity is not of immediate concern. The philosophical or reflective stance that the sceptic adopts is essentially one in which he becomes concerned with the question of the well-groundedness of our practice as a whole. Taking a disinterested or critical attitude towards our system of judgements, the sceptic is led to the apparent discovery that the judgements that form the framework of the system are really no more than presumptions, all of which rest on the unproved assumption that experience is a reliable guide to the nature of reality. On this view of it, it seems clear that as long as we do nothing to criticize the sceptic's assessment of the judgements of the frame, we can have no hope of a philosophical understanding of our ordinary practice that is in harmony with our ordinary outlook. It seems, therefore, that the best hope of a satisfactory reply to the sceptic lies in attempting to construct an account of our ordinary conviction in the judgements of the frame, which shows why the sceptic's belief that it stands everywhere in need of grounding or justification is wrong. What we want is an account that offers a non-sceptical interpretation of the lack of justification for the judgements that form the framework of our practice. Such an account would, on the one hand, reveal what is mistaken in the sceptic's own interpretation of ordinary practice (or of our system of judgements) as not well-grounded, and on the other, show why our commitment to the judgements of the frame is not dogmatic or presumptuous. By the same token, such an account would succeed in grounding Austin's methodological assumption that the investigation of 'what we should say when' is the investigation of the nature (or better, of the grammar) of phenomena.

The notion of objectivity will, on this approach, be something that we articulate through careful attention to the grammar of our concepts, or the distinctions that we draw within science and ordinary life. The question we will be concerned with, when we address the notion of objectivity, is which of our concepts represent ojective properties of the world, i.e. properties that it possesses independently of how it appears or presents itself to the characteristic perspective of human beings, and which of our concepts represent properties that the world possesses only in so far as it appears to a subject with a specific subjective constitution. The suggestion is that this distinction is one that we may discover through an examination of the grammatical differences between our concepts. For example, our concepts of colour reveal their relativity to the sensory equipment of the perceiver, i.e. reveal that they are concepts of phenomenal properties, in several ways. There is, for instance, no reduction of colour concepts to the non-phenomenal properties of objects; colour concepts do not figure in the causal explanation of physical phenomena; nor do they figure in the causal explanation of our perception of colour; the contrast between real and apparent colour is one that is drawn within experience; the notion of 'colour blindness' is not an idea of distorted perception of objects; and so on. By contrast, our concepts of shape reveal that they represent objective properties of the world, in the sense defined above, by virtue of the following grammatical features. The concept of shape is defined not in terms of how an object looks to a perceiver but in terms of the objective and measurable dispositions of its surface; the shape of an object figures in causal explanations of physical phenomena; the shape will also figure in a causal explanation of our perception of shape; the contrast between real and apparent shape is one between how the object looks to a perceiver and the objective disposition of its parts; the notion of 'shape blindness' (or stigmatism) is an idea of distorted perception of an object; and so on.

Given this notion of the objective properties of objects, we can say that a conception of the world is objective just in so far as it concerns itself with these properties and with the explanation of processes and phenomena in terms of them. The pursuit of an objective conception of the world, i.e. of a conception of the world as it is in itself, is simply the pursuit of a knowledge of what the world is like, how it developed, and what its processes are, in terms of concepts that attribute properties that objects possess intrinsically, independently of the perceiving subject and his specific subjective constitution. Such a conception of the world will abstract altogether from the question of how the world appears or feels, or what it means, or what its value is, to the human beings that inhabit it. Clearly, the objective conception of the world, as it is here understood, is not such as to invite scepticism regarding our ability to achieve objective knowledge of the world. Ojectivity is seen as a form of self-transcendence, but one that is quite plainly achievable, at least in principle. If scepticism troubles this conception of objectivity at all, it is only in the entirely general sense that we have not yet done the work of showing how it is that we have the right to this conception or to the implied optimism regarding our ability to achieve knowledge of the world.

Stroud's notion of objectivity is quite plainly different from the one that I have just outlined. He is not attempting to articulate a distinction among our concepts but to express a notion of how the world is that transcends any possible conception of it. For Stroud, the trouble with any notion of objectivity that emerges within our representations of the world is, presumably, precisely that it is *within* our representations, and is thus bounded by human subjectivity; it has not freed itself from all taint of the subjective. The point of this objection is expresssed clearly by Thomas Nagel as follows:

Objectivity and scepticism are closely related: both develop from the idea that there is a real world in which we are contained, and that appearances result from our interaction with the rest of it. We cannot accept those appearances uncritically, but must try to understand what our own constitution contributes to them. To do this we try to develop an idea of the world with ourselves in it, an account of both ourselves and the world that includes an explanation of why it initially appears to us as it does. But this idea, since it is we who develop it, is likewise the product of interaction between us and the world, though the interaction is more complicated and more self-conscious than the original one. If the initial appearances cannot be relied upon because they depend on our constitution in ways that we do not fully understand, this more complex idea should be open to the same doubts, for whatever we use to understand certain interactions between ourselves and the world is not itself the object of that understanding. However often we may try to step outside ourselves, something will have to stay behind the lens, something in us will determine the resulting picture, and this will give grounds for doubt that we are really getting any closer to reality.

The idea of objectivity thus seems to undermine itself. The aim is to form a conception of reality which includes ourselves and our view of things among its objects, but it seems that whatever forms the conception will not be included in it. It seems to follow that the most objective view we can achieve will have to rest on an unexamined subjective base, and that since we can never abandon our own point of view, but only alter it, the idea that we are coming closer to the reality outside it with each successive step has no foundation. (*The View From Nowhere*, pp. 67-8).

The concept of the objective world that emerges in connection with our ordinary distinction, implicit in the grammar of our concepts, between objective (or intrinsic) properties and properties that objects possess only in so far as they are present to a subject with a specific subjective constitution has, of course, no tendency to produce the idea of confinement that charaterizes Stroud's and Nagel's notion. Whatever content their concept of the objective world has, it is quite plainly not one that can be captured in terms of this ordinary distinction. In fact, I would like to suggest that the concept of objective reality that they are trying to express is actually a consequence, rather than the origin, of the sceptical argument. Thus, it is because the sceptic represents our framework judgements as knowledge claims that are presumptuous, in so far as they appear to rest on the unproved assumption that experience is a reliable guide to the nature of the objective world, that we are led to the idea of the possibility of a systematic distortion in the evidence on which our entire conception of the world is based. The sceptic makes us feel both that the objective judgements that form the frame of our practice require a justification, and that these judgements cannot be justified on the basis of experience, conceived purely subjectively. He is therefore able to create a sense that the starting point for all our beliefs imposes a limit that can never be transcended. In so far as we are led to seek a grounding for our entire system of judgements in something (experience) that is conceived independently of any presupposition that we are in touch with, or can know about, the objective world, the subjective nature of the alleged base makes it impossible for us to understand how it could support a system of objective knowledge. Thus, the notion of experience that emerges in the course of the sceptic's attempt to ground the objective judgements that form the frame of our practice serves to make self-transcendence seem impossible; the objective world (the world as it is for no subject) becomes something that we can only gesture at, as whatever lies (inconceivably) outside the limit of our own subjectivity.

Thus, the suggestion is that the concept of the objective world as something that is in principle beyond human knowledge depends on the sceptic's ability, first of all, to persuade us that the judgements of the frame need grounding, and then to lead us to a conception of the evidence for these judgements that inevitably creates a sense of restriction or confinement. It seems possible, therefore, that if we can show that the sceptic's assessment of the judgements of the frame as lacking a

justification they strictly require is mistaken, then the problematic conception of the evidence need never emerge, and the
associated sense of confinement need never be allowed to
develop. If we can provide an account that reveals why the
objective judgements of the frame constitute a legitimate, non-
presumptuous starting point, then we shall be in a position to
avoid opening up a gap through which the notion of possibly
misleading evidence, or potential distortion, could enter.
Moreover, we should have at least provided a climate in which a
conception of subjectivity that keeps us in touch with the world
of public objects could be constructed. By the same token, we
should no longer need to construe the concept of the objective
world in such a way as to provide a goal for the sceptic's
unfulfilled concept of objective knowledge. The objective
world becomes the familiar world, or the ordinary objects we
experience, described or conceived independently of our own
peculiar sensory and emotional perspective.

It is perhaps worth noting here that this difference in
approach to the problem of scepticism implies an entirely
different conception of the nature of philopsophy. For both
Stroud and Nagel, what is distinctive of philosophy is its desire
to address itself to the above problematic conception of the
objective world; philosophy is concerned with understanding
something about ourselves but from a self-transcendent, or
God's eye, point of view. It is for this reason that philosophy is
seen as an essentially *critical* discipline: what we appear to
discover from the objectively superior perspective may well
force us to recognize a weakness, or egocentricity, in our
position of which we were previously unaware . On the current
conception, the task of philosophy is to provide an understanding of the workings of the phenomenon of human practice. In
so far as the phenomenon we are attempting to understand is
something in which we also participate, the task is necessarily a
reflective one: we must temporarily put off engagement in
order to stand back and attempt the task of constructing an
account. The enterprise is not essentially a critical one, but is
rather an attempt simply to understand an independent,
natural phenomenon in a way that makes it intelligible to us. It
is this view of philosophy that makes both scepticism and the

bare reaffirmation of common-sense appear so unsatisfactory, for plainly neither achieves the understanding that should, I am suggesting, be our aim. That is, neither provides an account of human practice that allows us to understand why we (already) have the right to proceed in the way that we do.

5

On The Significance of What We Would Ordinarily Claim to Know

In this chapter I will look at another attempt to undermine the sceptic's argument, which involves, as a central part, detailed observations on the way in which the traditional epistemologist's employment of the words 'I know' is, from the point of view of ordinary practice, deviant. The argument I want to consider is given by Stanley Cavell, in *The Claim of Reason*. One reason that I want to consider Cavell's argument is that, while he shares Austin's view that there is something fatally deviant in the traditional epistemologist's use of words, he also believes that neither the fact that the epistemologist's use of epistemic terms is to a certain extent novel, nor the fact that the epistemologist's use of these terms leads him to draw a conclusion that is in direct conflict with what we would ordinarily take to be the case, can on its own establish this. Cavell is, if you like, aware of the need to avoid the methodological dogmatism implicit in any attempt to use observations about how words are normally used as 'direct criticism' of the sceptic's argument. Cavell believes that in order to be successful our criticism of the traditional epistemologist's enquiry must include some precise and detailed explanation of just how the epistemologist's assertions stray into unintelligibility, and of how it is that they can nevertheless *appear*, in a philosophical context, so natural and compelling. Cavell's approach, therefore, seems to offer fresh hope of our achieving the sort of philosophical understanding I have suggested is vital to a satisfactory rebuttal of the sceptic.

Cavell's initial view of the sceptic's argument is very much the one taken here. He believes that the sceptic's reflections strike us as natural, compelling and unanswerable; that the conclusion of these reflections is in outright conflict with what we ordinarily take to be the case; and that sceptic's conclusion is entirely powerless to bring conviction or undermine our commitment to common sense. Furthermore, Cavell also shares my view that the remoteness of scepticism from ordinary life does not constitute, and cannot immediately yield, a satisfactory ground for rejecting the sceptic's argument. He believes that the epistemologist's ability to lead us by the nose to a sense of *discovering* that we ought not to enter or accept knowledge claims that we do ordinarily accept makes any insistence that the epistemologist has 'misused language', or 'changed the meaning of our words', hollow and unsatisfactory. The power of the sceptic's reflections to drive us along willy nilly to the sceptical conclusion appears to show that the argument relies on nothing that is not part of our ordinary understanding of the key epistemic terms, and facts of normal usage on their own do nothing to counter this impression. For Cavell too, therefore, a genuine resolution of the tension between the unliveability and the unanswerability of scepticism cannot simply use the former as a reason to reject the sceptic's conclusion, but awaits a much deeper understanding of what has gone wrong with the sceptic's reasoning.

Cavell sums up his view of scepticism in *The Claim of Reason* as follows:

> Let me . . . emphasise what I take the sense of discovery to indicate about the philosopher's conclusion. First, since it is a discovery whose content is that something we have, supposedly, all believed has been shown to be false or superstitious or in some respect suspect, its sense of being a discovery depends upon a sense of its *conflicting* with what we would all, supposedly, have said we knew or thought. And this sense of conflict depends upon the words which express the conclusion meaning or seeming

to mean what these words, as ordinarily used, would express. For *that* is what the conclusion conflicts with. (Ibid., p. 164)

He goes on:

> Second, the philosopher's conclusion seems, in this conflict, to be right, and indeed to be deeper than our everyday, average ideas . . . [T]he convincingness of the conclusion depend[s] upon its proceeding, or seeming to proceed, in just the ordinary way an ordinary person must (grammatically) proceed to establish a claim to know of something's existence . . . The Cartesian epistemologist, we might say, is not impugning ordinary *methods* of supporting or assesing knowledge, but rather feels himself to have shown that in our ordinary employment of these methods we are not normally careful or precise enough. (Ibid.,p. 165)

Nevertheless, the philosopher's enquiry is sufficiently extraordinary that 'a method which ordinarily yields unworried conviction turn(s) out to yield , in the philosopher's hands, a conclusion whose conviction will not detach from the context of investigation itself' (Ibid., p. 165).

For Cavell, therefore, some sort of understanding is needed in addition to a knowledge of how the words 'I know' are normally used. This further understanding must convince us of what the ordinary language philosopher in a sense assumes, namely that in failing to use words as we normally do (fully naturally), the traditional epistemologist fails to mean what he thinks he means by the words he utters; indeed, fails to speak in such a way as to make him worth listening to at all. What Cavell thinks we must show is that the traditional epistemologist's particular projection of our normal procedures for entering and assessing knowledge claims is such that either we cannot properly be said to understand him, or, if we do understand him, we cannot derive the sceptical conclusion from what he says. In order to achieve this, Cavell thinks we need to command a much clearer view of what a word means, of, what it is to mean something by uttering a word, of what it is to understand what someone's words mean, and of what it is to understand what someone means by uttering the words he does.

A second reason for being interested in Cavell's argument is that it focuses its attack on scepticism at a quite different point from Austin. Cavell's argument concentrates on the idea that there is something suspect in the *initial claims to know* – 'I know that this is a hand (sheet of paper, pen, desk, chair, table, tomato, etc.)' – with which the traditional epistemologist's enquiry invariably begins. Thus, Cavell's question is not so much whether the sceptic's ground for doubt is fully legitimate but rather whether the examples of knowledge claims with which the sceptic's enquiry gets off the ground are fully intelligible. Cavell's idea is that once the sort of knowledge claim on which the sceptic's enquiry is based has been entered, then the sceptic's doubts, which would not even delay us in a normal context, come to seem both relevant and fatal to our ability to know. Whatever oddness the sceptic's doubt has is, therefore, to be understood via an understanding of the oddness of the claim against which it is raised, for it is there, Cavell believes, that the infection begins. Once we have been led into considering, say, the judgement that this is a hand as a claim to knowledge then we can do nothing to prevent the sceptic's conclusion from seeming inevitable; no attempt to show that the grounds for doubt are odd can fully succeed once the knowledge claim itself has been allowed; it is the nature of the knowledge claim that lends to the doubt precisely the air of naturalness on which the power of sceptic's argument depends. What we need to understand, therefore, is the precise way in which the traditional epitemologist strays into unintelligibility by introducing, in the sort of context he does introduce it, a claim to know 'This is a hand'.

Cavell's argument begins with careful reflection on the significance of the difference between the examples of knowledge claims from which Austin derives his observations on what is requisite for knowledge and the examples of knowldege claims which characteristically preface the sceptic's argument. Austin's examples always involve objects – goldfinches, woodpeckers, bitterns, etc. – for which all of the following are true:

1 There is a real question whether the object has been *identified* (i.e. assigned to its kind) correctly.
2 The idea of someone's having the necessary *expertise* to identify the object correctly makes sense.
3 In making the identification of the object someone could be supplying *genuine information* to his audience.

Cavell labels objects meeting these three conditions 'Austinian object', or 'specific objects'. It is, Cavell believes, a matter of immense significance that the knowledge claims with which the traditional epistemologist's enquiry begins *never* involve Austinian objects. Cavell suggests that, given a knowledge claim involving an Austinian object, the ubiquitously relevant question, 'How do you know?', has one of two natural interpretations: (a) 'By means of what features can you tell?' (b) 'What relevant training/expertise do you have that puts you in a specially good position for identifying objects of this sort?' The important point is that, interpreted in either of these ways, the question 'How do you know?' appears entirely unproblematic. We know in either case what it would be to satisfy the request to state how we know; sceptical difficulties simply never crop up to threaten our ability to sustain the claim.

Cavell's suggestion is that, by taking examples of knowledge claims involving Austinian objects, Austin makes his decription of what is requisite for knowledge (in particular, the 'enough-is-enough'-condition) appear inevitable and quite correct. Given the nature of Austin's examples, the problem of whether we know that our description of the object is correct is naturally construed as a problem of knowing whether we have identified (are in a position to identify) the object correctly. The problem of how we know whether the object *really exists* is, given the sort of claim we are looking at, strained and unnatural; we recognize these claims as ones made in a context in which the problem of how we know the object really exists does not arise. 'Austin takes a case in which, as he says, you (can) have provided enough to show that there is "no room for an alternative competing description of it". This is the case in which the *problem* of knowledge is one, and initially one solely, of correct description (identification, recognition)' (ibid.,

p. 52). Cavell's point is that this is *not* the problem of knowledge as it occurs for the traditional epistemologist. He believes that this comes out immediately when we turn our attention to the sorts of objects that invariably figure in the examples of knowledge claims on which the traditional epistemologist's enquiry focuses. When we look at the epistemologist's examples, we cannot but acknowledge that he is no longer concerned with the problem of knowing that we have identified the object correctly, but precisely with the problem of knowing whether the object really exists, which seemed unnatural and remote in the case of claims involving Austinian objects.

The objects that figure in the traditional epistemologist's claims – hands, tables, chairs, desks, pieces of paper, pens, etc. – are such that 1-3 above are *never* true of them, or at least never true of them in the sort of context in which the epistemologist introduces his claim, i.e. when they are close at hand, in full view, in a good light, etc. These 'generic objects', as Cavell labels them, are all 'ones specifically about which there just is no problem of recognition or identification or description' (ibid., p. 52). Once a claim involving a generic object has been entered – the claim, say, that this is a hand – the logic of our language makes the question 'How do you know?' inevitable. But now, given that there can be no real question either of identification or expertise, we cannot but be led into interpreting the question as raising a problem that makes us immediately prey to the sceptic. Thus, given that it makes no sense to interpret the 'How do you know?' question as meaning either 'By means of what features have you identified this object as correctly describable by the word "hand"?', or 'What special training/expertise do you have that puts you in a specially good position for identifying objects of this sort?', we are pushed into interpreting it as follows: 'How do you know that this object *really exists*?'. And once we have been led into interpreting the 'How do you know?' question this way, the sceptic's reflections suddenly appear both relevant and entirely fatal to our ability to sustain the claim. Cavell writes:

In the sense in which it is obviously unreasonable to ask of a specific (i.e. Austinian) object, without a special reason for asking, whether my basis for claiming to know (e.g. 'From the red head') is enough to show it is real – in that sense it is *not* unreasonable to ask of a generic object, granted that it has presented itself as a problem of knowledge, whether our basis for claiming to know (typically 'I see it'; 'I know it by means of the senses') is enough to show that it is real. (Ibid., p. 55)

However, is is not merely that the sceptic's reflections appear to be fatal to my ability to sustain the claim to know that this is a hand, but that, again in virtue of the nature of the generic object, it is fatal to *anyone's* ability to sustain *any* knowledge claim involving *any* external object whatever. If a claim to know what sort of object an Austinian object is fails, this failure has no tendency to move out and infect all other knowledge claims involving Austinian objects; it remains completely specific to the claim under discussion. If it turns out that the red head is a trick of the light, or that the bird flies away before I have a chance to check, or even if it proves that my expertise is just not up to providing reliable identifications of types of bird, this does not generally impugn the fact that sometimes people are sufficiently expert, the light sufficiently good and the bird still long enough to ensure that a correct identification has been made. By contrast, when the sceptic shows that I am not, given my inability to rule out the sceptical hypotheses, in a position to claim to know that this is a hand, he thereby appears to demonstrate that *no one ever knows that anything really exists*. The featurelessness of generic objects, and the lack of an appropriate notion of expertise, make it clear that is nothing about *me*, or *my* position, or even about *this* object that makes it impossible to sustain a knowledge claim; a claim made by *anyone*, in *any* position, involving *any* generic object would, we perceive, be in exactly the same boat. It is, in other words, in virtue of the fact that the traditional epistemologist's claims involve generic objects that the sceptical conclusion has a tendency to become entirely general. Cavell puts it like this:

It is, I have said, of the essence of the traditional epistemologist's investigations that the objects he uses as examples are not ones about which there is something more to learn in the way of recognising them; *no one's position*, with respect to identifying them, *is better than anyone else's*. An island of earth is faced by an island of consciousness, of sense experience. And this proves not to be enough for knowing. The epistemologist's question can be formulated as 'How do *we* know, e.g., that . . . ?', and the question this turns out to investigate is 'How do we know (can we be certain) that *anything* exists?'. (Ibid., p. 56)

It is the nature of the claim that the traditional epistemologist investigates, that lends to the sceptic's doubt whatever naturalness it has, and that makes it possible for the sceptic to derive a general conclusion about our inability to know external facts from the examination of a single case. Thus, a proper diagnosis of what has gone amiss when we find ourselves unable to put a stop to the sceptic's argument should focus on the claims that the traditional epistemologist investigates, for once this point is past the sceptic cannot, without an appearance of dogmatism, be halted. Cavell's approach, therefore, is to try to persuade us that we cannot attach any real meaning to knowledge claims involving generic objects, and hence that the sceptic's argument fails before it even gets off the ground. However, as I emphasized earlier, the unintelligibility of the claim that the epistemologist investigates is not to be established either by pointing out that we never, in the course of ordinary practice, make knowledge claims of that sort, or by insisting on the absurdity of the conclusion to which the traditional epistemologist's investigation inevitably leads. Rather, we are to be provided with an understanding of what it is to say something and mean something by it, which will allow us to see *why* the philosopher fails to mean anything by the words he utters when he introduces the claim that he investigates, and *how* he (and we) could have failed to see that this is so.

Cavell's suggestion about the way in which the traditional epistemologist fails to mean anything by the sort of knowledge claim he characteristically investigates depends crucially on the distinction between what a particular word or sentence means and *what someone means by uttering* a particular word or sentence. What a word means is 'what any good dictionary tells us it means', what any adequate definition of the words must state. In this sense of 'means' we might think of the English language as consisting of a very large number of expressions, each with a specific cataloguable meaning, which can be put together in numerous ways to form new, more complex, expressions, some of which will be whole sentences, which in turn possess specific meanings in this sense. But aside from this notion of what a word or expression means, there is also a notion of meaning that relates to the actual *use* of expression, on specific occasions, in *acts* of assertion. The latter idea of meaning is essentially the idea of *speakers* meaning something *by* uttering the words they do. Cavell's fundamental point is not that speakers mean (or often mean) something other than what their words mean but that understanding what a speaker means on a particular occasion requires more than recognizing what his words mean, in the first sense of 'mean'; it requires that we understand the *point* of his saying what he does. Moreover, the point of a speaker's act of assertion cannot be determined merely from his words (the meaning of his words) alone, but depends on our being able to see his utterance as an act made intelligible by the context of ends, interests, motives, etc. in which it is embedded. It is only if his utterance can thus be construed as the intelligible action of a rational human agent that a *speaker* succeeds in meaning anything at all by what he utters.

Cavell argues that philosophers have failed to see how the traditional epistemologist has 'emptied his words of meaning' because the history of philosophy is a 'history of . . . concentration on the meaning of particular words and sentences in isolation from a systematic attention to their concrete uses' (Ibid., pp. 206–7). By looking for meaning exclusively in the region of what words or sentences mean, philosophers have failed to see that one important way of meaning nothing is for the point of our saying the words we do to be lost. The traditional way of thinking about meaning has led philosophers to neglect the fact that 'to know what a person has said you have to know that he or she has *asserted* something, and know what he or she has asserted' (ibid., p. 208). This in turn has allowed the philosopher to ignore the question of the point of utterances made in a philosophical context, and made him blind to one crucial way in which the epistemologist's utterances might stray into unintelligibility. The philosopher's false assumption that it is the meaning of our words (in the first sense of 'meaning') that secures what *we* mean by them has made it impossible for him to discover that

> 'Not saying anything' is one way philosophers do not know what they mean. In this case it is not that they mean something *other* than they say, but that they do not see that they mean nothing (that *they* mean nothing, not that their statements mean nothing, are nonsense). (Ibid., p. 210)

Cavell's attempt to show that the knowledge claims that the philosopher investigates are illegitimate or unintelligible is thus an attempt to show, not that the words that the philosopher utters in introducing these claims are themselves meaningless, but that, given the context in which he utters them, we cannot see the point of his saying them, we cannot see what *he* means by them, we cannot construe his utterance of them as an intelligible act of assertion.

The crucial idea, therefore, is that there are two distinct notions of meaning – word-meaning and speaker's-meaning – that are linked together in a much more complex way than the traditional philosopher has supposed. The relationship between these two concepts may be illuminated by means of Davidson's proposal concerning the construction of a systematic theory of meaning for a radically foreign language, L. (See Davidson, *Inquiries into Truth and Interpretation*, especially essays 9 and 10.) The aim of a systematic theory of meaning for L is to enable the radical interpreter to arrive at content-specifying descriptions of the acts of assertion performed by speakers of L. The data on which the interpreter bases his theory relate to the attitude of 'holding-true' strings of phonemes, manifest by speakers of L, in specific, observable circumstances. The interpreter, Davidson suggests, arrives at a theory of meaning for L on the basis of this data by, on the one hand, imposing a logical grammar on the strings of phonemes, and on the other, assigning interpretations to the non-logical expressions of L, in such a way that speakers of L come out holding-true sentences of L that are true, by the interpreter's lights, as often as possible. Once a systematic theory meeting these constraints has been constructed, then the interpreter can use it to determine what a speaker has asserted by the utterance, on a specific occasion, of a particular sentence s of L. Cavell's view of the relationship between word- meaning and speaker's-meaning might now be expressed as the claim that it is a mistake to suppose that the task of interpreting others can ever be taken over completely by the systematic theory of meaning for L. In particular, a speaker's uttering a given sentence, s, to which the theory of meaning assigns the interpretation, p, is never a guarantee that the speaker is correctly described as having performed the act of asserting p.

What Cavell is suggesting is, in a sense, that the *interpreter's* role in interpreting others continues even after a systematic theory of meaning has been constructed; there is, if you like, no systematic, rule-governed route from knowing what is assigned by the theory as meaning to the expressions of L to understanding what has been asserted by a speaker of L on a given occasion of utterance. For the interpreter can never put off altogether the need to satisfy himself that the content-specifying description of the act of assertion that the systematic theory yields makes this particular utterance, in these particular concrete circumstances, intelligible to him as the act of a human agent participating in a humanly recognizable form of life. Normally, of course, all will go smoothly – that is the criterion of a successful theory – but the continuing role of the interpreter becomes apparent in those, necessarily rare, cases where the theory, in a sense, fails us. In a case where the theory yields a description of a speaker's act of uttering a sentence s of L as the act of asserting p, and the interpreter is simply unable to see how, in this context, the act of asserting p could constitute the intelligible act of a human agent, then the interpreter must supplement the theory with *ad hoc* explanations. At these points the interpreter must resort to hypotheses about deviations of idiolect ('He means *imply* by "infer"'), failures of understanding ('He doesn't know what the word "pusillanimous" means'), failures of hearing ('I must have misheard "ninety" for "nineteen"'), or, more drastically, failures of sanity ('He must be mad'). All this is only meant to bring out in a clear way that understanding speakers is *always* more than knowing what meaning a systematic theory of meaning for their language assigns to their words; the interpreter's need to see the point of what a speaker is doing in asserting a given proposition is a never-ending and ineliminable contribution to the task of understanding others; the task of understanding *speakers* is always something more than knowing a theory of meaning for their language.

The importance of this point for Cavell's undermining of scepticism is that it allows Cavell to claim that although a systematic theory of meaning for English would assign an interpretation to the words 'I know that this is a hand', the particular utterance of these words by the traditional epistemologist does not allow us, as interpreters, to satisfy ourselves that we can understand his utterance as an intelligible act of asserting that he knows that this is a hand. Cavell argues that if we look at the circumstances in which the epistemologist introduces the claim, then we shall have to acknowledge that we cannot see the point of an act of asserting 'I know that this is a hand', and we shall be obliged to resort to some sort of *ad hoc* explanation of his utterance. The explanation Cavell favours, clearly, is that there is a very subtle failure of understanding on the traditional epistemologist's part. It is not that he does not know what meaning the theory of meaning for English assigns to the words 'I know that this is a hand', but that he temporarily (while doing philosophy) overlooks the fact that not just anything counts as making an assertion; he forgets that asserting has its conditions, that one of these conditions is that the assertions have a point, and that his assertion of 'I know that this is a hand' has none.

Let us consider, then, the sort of claim that the traditional epistemologist characteristically investigates, for instance the claim 'I know that this is a hand'. It is, of course, crucial to the traditional epistemologist's purpose that there should be nothing in the circumstances in which he introduces this claim either that makes the fact that the given object is a hand especially remarkable or noteworthy, or that puts the speaker in a superior position for recognizing that the object is a hand. The epistemologist's desire to investigate a 'best case' of a knowledge claim, Cavell argues, motivates him to select an object for which no real question of identification (and therefore of misidentification), or of expertise (and therefore lack of expertise) in identifying, can arise. It is crucial to the traditional epistemologist's whole enterprise that he investigates a claim in which any discovered inability to sustain the claim does not arise from a weakness *peculiar* to the particular claim being investigated, but only from a completely general incapacity to know how things stand in reality. It is the epistemologist's interest in knowledge in general that leads him exclusively to consider claims involving what Cavell has labelled 'generic objects'. As far as the epistemologist is concerned, therefore, only a knowledge claim that is 'flamingly obvious' to everyone, whose assertion or remark would normally have *no* point, will serve his purpose. The real work that still remains to be done is the work of persuading us that just because there would ordinarily be no point in asserting, in the sort of circumstances in which the traditional epistemologist asserts it, 'I know that this is a hand', we really cannot understand his utterance as an intelligible act of assertion at all.

Cavell suggests that the most likely form of objection to the idea that attempting to assert a knowledge claim which would ordinarily have no point results in a mere empty mouthing of words is best expressed as follows:

Perhaps one feels: 'What difference does it make that no one would have *said*, without a special reason for saying it, that you know [that this is a hand]? You *did* know it; it's *true* to say you knew it. Are you suggesting that one sometimes cannot say what is true?' (Ibid., pp. 205–6)

'But', someone will . . . feel, '[the epistemologist's] statements are *true*, and it is outrageous to say that they "cannot" be said. Surely you can simply *remark* something without that being something the person may not have known.' (Ibid ., p. 210)

'The only oddness or unnaturalness in saying ["He knows that this is a hand"] is just that it is so flamingly *obvious* that he knows, and if you're going to try to convince us that just because it is odd in *that* sense, that therefore we cannot or ought not to say it, then you're trying to convince us that we cannot or ought not say something which is true, true in spades. And that is just outrageous.' (Ibid., p. 211)

The main thrust of Cavell's argument against the intelligibility of the knowledge claims that the sceptic investigates is, therefore, directed towards countering the belief that uttering a meaningful sentence that is true is enough to constitute one's utterance as an intelligible act of assertion; that his words have a meaning and that the proposition they express is true is not, Cavell argues, enough to ensure that the *speaker* can mean something by uttering the words he does. The argument is as follows.

In order for an utterance to be an intelligible act of assertion it is, as a matter of 'logic' or 'grammar', essential that the act have some recognizable point; a pointless utterance (Wittgenstein's disconnected 'Down with him!', *On Certainty*, 350) cannot be an intelligible act of assertion. The suggestion that whatever is true can be meaningfully said or asserted amounts, therefore, to a claim that something's being true is always enough to give the assertion of it a point, is always enough to constitute a *reason* for asserting it. Cavell's argument against the intelligibility of the sceptic's claim is that '"Because it is true" is *not* a reason or basis for saying anything, it does not constitute the point of your saying something; and I am suggesting that there must, in grammar, be reasons for what you say, or be a point in your saying something, if what you say is to be comprehensible' (ibid., p. 206). If truth could constitute a reason for assertion, then an individual who goes round endlessly enumerating perfectly obvious facts – 'That's a chair. I know that's a chair. That's a table. I know that's a table. That's an ashtray. I know that's an ashtray . . . ' – ought to make sense to us when clearly he does not. The claim the epistemologist considers is, as Cavell sees it, as unintelligible as those of the obsessive babbler: neither can be construed as a rational human agent engaged in an intelligible form of human action. The idea of the obsessive babbler forces us to recognize that truth alone cannot be a *reason* to act; endlessly remarking the obvious results only in incoherence; there is ceaseless chatter, but that is all; the speaker himself has altogether ceased to be intelligible to us. At the same time it forces us to recognize how far the philosopher strays into incoherence and unintelligibility: the philosopher appears to perform an act of entering a knowledge claim, but in fact he has no more reason for what he does, his behaviour is no more an *act* of assertion, than in the case of the obsessive babbler. It is because the philosopher utters words in a context in which there *can* be no reason for saying them that Cavell believes his saying of them cannot be correctly described as an *act* of asserting at all; all there is is the mere empty mouthing of the words 'I know that this is a hand': *'no concrete claim is ever entered as part of the traditional investigation'* (ibid., p. 217).

Cavell goes on to reinforce his argument against the sceptic by posing a dilemma for the traditional epistemologist. He has argued that saying something and meaning something by it depends on the saying's being construable as the intelligible act of a rational human agent. To think of meaning something in this way is immediately to concretize it, or embed it in the particular circumstances that form the background to it and render it intelligible in this sense. A saying's constituting an intelligible act of assertion requires that it serve some recognizable point *given* the physical circumstances, the interests, beliefs, etc. of the speaker, and so on: acts are necessarily embedded in a context of motives, ends, physical circumstances, etc. which provide the *reasons* for acting, and constitute physical behaviour as rational action. The argument given above, against the intelligibility of the claim that the traditional epistemologist considers, suggests that the epistemologist's utterance of the words 'I know that this is a hand' cannot be thus construed as an intelligible act of assertion; there is nothing in the circumstances of utterance that can provide the necessary matrix of ends and means. Cavell now argues that if the sceptic responds to this criticism by insisting that the claim he investigates is made intelligible by the context of philosophical concern that provokes him to introduce it, then any objection that can be raised against the claim will merely be an objection to this particular concrete claim, from which no general conclusion concerning the sustainability, or otherwise, of *all* knowledge claims can possibly be derived. If the claim that the sceptic investigates is thought of as the contextualized claim of a particular rational agent, made in quite specific circumstances, then it can no longer serve as a *representative* for all possible knowledge claims, and can, therefore, no longer yield the general sceptical conclusion. It becomes, as it were, like all other knowledge claims, isolated in its particularity. Thus

> The 'dilemma' the traditional investigation of knowledge is involved in may now be formulated in this way: it must be the investigation of a concrete claim if its procedure is to be coherent; it cannot be the investigation of a concrete claim if its conclusion is to be general. Without that coherence it would not have the obviousness it has seemed to have; without that generality its conclusion would not be sceptical. (Ibid., p. 220)

For Cavell, therefore, the whole power of the sceptic's argument to generate a general conclusion about the possibility of knowledge depends on its being empty in just the way described above. The attempt to produce a claim that is secure against any *specific* weakness, and thus able to serve as a representative for all knowledge, has led the philosopher into making an utterance that defies interpretation as an *act* of claiming to know: meaninglessness is, as it were, endemic to the philosopher's extraordinary investigation.

One advantage of Cavell's suggestion that the claim the sceptic considers is possessed of this quite specific sort of unintelligibility is that it serves to deepen our understanding of *why* the sceptic's claim leads inexorably to the sceptical conclusion. Deprived of meaning, in the sense of what the *speaker* means by uttering the words 'I know that this is a hand', we are left only with what the words mean. We are left, in other words, with meaning in a sense that has no connection with the normal forms of human activity and practical enquiry, but is simply an abstracted, unengaged potential. Left with this purely abstract notion of meaning, we cannot but experience a powerlessness to settle the truth of the claim 'I know that this is a hand'. The words are no longer being *used* by a human agent, in the course of human practice, to *do* something; there are merely the words and what they mean. Inevitably, therefore, the question 'How do you know?' gets divorced from the *practical* questions 'How did you indentify the object? What special training do you have that puts you into a position to indentify this object as correctly describable in the way you have described it?' The question has to be interpreted in a manner that is as abstract as the meaning we are left with: How do you know whether this purely abstract meaning matches or mirrors an equally abstract notion of the world? Interpreted in this way, the question clearly cannot be settled by the ordinary, practical methods that human beings employ in settling questions concerning concrete, practical claims to know. The question no longer belongs to the familiar, practical world in which human beings act and make decisions but to a purely abstract realm. It cannot be settled by us but depends on the relationship between two entirely abstract entities. This is the muddle into which we are led by neglecting the fact that for a speaker to mean something is a form of *action*, which, like all other forms of action, has the (grammatical) constraint of intelligibility on it.

Cavell's argument is an attempt, therefore, to show that the universal constraint of intelligibility limits us to operating within the normal forms of human action; the philosopher's attempt to perform an act of assertion without meeting the demands on normal human action results in something that is, as it were, beyond the bounds of sense. The argument is intended to show us why we do not need to hearken to the sceptic's argument, why the argument does not constitute a genuine criticism of ordinary practice; for it exposes the sceptic's words as entirely empty or idle. At first sight, therefore, Cavell's reflections appear to achieve our objective of revealing the sceptic's criticisms as worthless and earning our commitment to unqualified common sense. However, I have all along insisted that a satisfactory resolution of scepticism must avoid all need to beg the question of the truth of our ordinary judgments against the sceptic. The question we now need to address ourselves to, therefore, is whether Cavell's alleged exposure of the form of unintelligibility that afflicts the traditional epistemologist succeeds in avoiding any dogmatic assumption that our ordinary judgments are for the most part true.

The stage of Cavell's argument we need to focus on is, I believe, the one at which he tries to bring out that we cannot, in the context, understand the point of the epistemologist's claim to know that this is a hand. It is absolutely crucial to Cavell's mode of demostrating that we cannot really see an intelligible point to the philosopher's knowledge claim, that we begin by agreeing that the fact which the philosopher claims to know is, in his words, 'flamingly obvious'. Thus, as we saw earlier, he represents the traditional epistemologist's objection to the suggestion that he cannot intelligibly make his claim as follows:

> Perhaps one feels: 'What difference does it make that no one would have *said*, without a special reason for saying it, that you know [that *this* is a hand]? You did know it; it's *true* to say you knew it. Are you suggesting that one sometimes cannot say what is true?'

> But some will . . . feel, '[The epistemologist's] statements are *true*, and it is outrageous to say that they "cannot" be said.'

> 'you're trying to convince us that we cannot or ought not to say something which is true, true in spades. And that is outrageous.'

It is crucial to this particular strand of Cavell's argument that the epistemologist should defend his introduction of, e.g., the claim 'I know that this is a hand' in this way, by insisting that whatever is true can meaningfully be said, because Cavell's ultimate rejection of the claim as empty depends on his demonstrating that a statement's being true is never enough to constitute asserting it as the intelligible act of a rational human agent. Thus, the argument against the legitimacy of the claim that the epistemologist considers depends on the assumption that he is incapable, in the context, of motivating the claim 'I know that this is a hand' as an *interesting* claim, as a claim concerning which its truth may be in question. Moreover, it requires that the epistemologist himself, at the moment of introducing the claim, shares our essentially common-sense attitude that the claim is obviously true, that it is, in an important sense, not worth making. Once Cavell has got the traditional epistemologist to concede all this, then he is in a position to use his reflections on the act of assertion and the constraints on intelligible action to show that there is no reason to make the claim; that the act of claiming does not meet the conditions for performing an act; that the epistemologist has, in effect, uttered words quite idly, without asserting anything at all.

It seems clear, therefore, that Cavell's demonstration that the claim the epistemologist investigates is unintelligible depends on a willingness on the epistemologist's part to accept that when he puts forward the claim, 'I know that this is a hand', he shares our ordinary assessment of the embedded judgement as obviously correct. It is only if the epistemologist takes the attitude that the embedded judgement is undoubtedly and incontrovertibly true, that the claim can be shown by Cavell to be unmotivated and unintelligible. And it does seem that, given this starting point, Cavell's demonstration of the emptiness of the claim is quite correct, for if we imagine a context in which our ordinary attitude of conviction prevails – e.g. within ordinary practice – then we see immediately that someone's making the claim 'I know that this is a hand' would, without special reason, be odd to the point of incoherence. Furthermore, it seems that the epistemologist's alleged interest in a 'best case' of a knowledge claim, i.e. one in which there are no real questions of identification or expertise, ensures that the epistemologist must be willing to accept that he chooses a claim that he regards, at the time of introducing it, as quite beyond doubt. However, despite all this, it seems to me that there is good reason to question Cavell's characterization of the traditional epistemologist's positon, on which the whole force of his rebuttal depends.

In chapter 1 I argued that the sceptic's argument should be understood as having seven discernible stages, which I characterized as follows:

1 The sceptic takes up a *reflective stance vis-à-vis* our ordinary practice of making and accepting knowledge claims.
2 He observes that he has fallen into error in the past and undertakes the *critical examination* of his current claims to know.
3 He discovers that they are made within a *framework of judgements*, which he implicitly claims to know, but which he has never justfied.
4 He formulates a *project of justification* regarding the judgements of the frame.
5 He uncovers an *unproved assumption* lying behind his acceptance of the frameword judgements.
6 He constructs the *Sceptical Hypotheses* which reveal that the general assumption cannot, without circularity, be justified.
7 He concludes that there should be *complete suspension of judgement* concerning the nature of the objective world.

On this account of the argument, the introduction of the claim 'I know that this is a hand' occurs only in the *fourth* stage of the argument, when the sceptic addresses himself to the project of justifying a (now explicit) claim to know a representative judgement of the frame. The sceptic's interest in introducing and attempting to justify the claim 'I know that this is a hand' has, therefore, been motivated by the general reflections which preface the introduction of the claim and which serve to reveal it as standing in need of critical examination. These preliminary reflections serve, if you like, to achieve the suspension of precisely the attitude of commitment to the judgements that normally form the framework of our practice, from which Cavell's demonstration of the unintelligibility of the claim requires us to start . The traditional epistemologist has, as it were, made his ordinary attitude of commitment a question for himself, in order to discover whether he can genuinely earn his conviction that his view of the world, as it is expressed in these judgements, is, by and large, correct. Thus, the idea is that the first three stages of the sceptic's reflections are vital, for they serve to motivate a general refusal to concede our common- sense attitude that the truth of 'This is a hand', or 'I know that this is a hand', is 'flamingly obvious'. The introduction of the claim 'I know that this is a hand', is motivated in turn by the sense of a need to discover whether a representative knowledge claim concerning a judgement of the frame can be given the (apparently) requisite justification. The traditional epistemologist is, therefore, quite unlike the madman who walks around enumerating perfectly obvious facts. For the madman *is* remarking what he knows to be 'flamingly obvious', out of some sort of pathological obsessiveness; the propositions that the madman utters have not, through the contemplative suspension of our common-sense attitude, previously become a question for him; there is nothing that gives his expression of these judgements an intelligible point.

On the current view of it, therefore, Cavell is quite wrong to regard the traditional epistemologist's enquiry as *initiated* by a knowledge claim involving a generic object. Indeed, I think it is his need to make the introduction of the knowledge claim the start of the enquiry that prevents Cavell from offering any very convincing account of the origin of scepticism. The sceptic's knowledge claim has to be made without any prior suspension of our ordinary attitude of commitment, completely out of the blue, otherwise Cavell's method for exposing it as illegitimate cannot work. On Cavell's account of the sceptic's argument, it is very difficult to see why the epistemologist should have introduced the claim in the first place, or why, once it had been introduced, it was not simply ignored, as the madman's claims are ignored in everyday life.

However, it might now be objected, on Cavell's behalf, that if I have succeeded in motivating the epistemologist's introduction of the claim, 'I know that this is a hand', then we have simply landed ourselves on the second horn of Cavell's final dilemma. If the epistemologist's claim is a genuine claim, well motivated in the context, then we cannot derive any general conclusion concerning our inability to sustain claims to know about the objective world from it. However, I feel that this alternative objection to the sceptic's argument has really very little power to persuade, for it is hard to see why a claim, motivated in the way I have suggested, cannot serve as a representative case. The claim is, I have argued, motivated by an entirely general doubt regarding the justifiability of our ordinary attitude of commitment to the truth of a mass of judgements that form the background of our practice. The claim is chosen precisely because we are able to recognize that it offers the best possible circumstances in which to test our ability to sustain an explicit claim to know a judgement of the frame and show that our system of belief is well-grounded.

The claim, 'I know that this is a hand', is able to serve as a representative claim, first of all, because of the general nature of the doubt that makes it a claim worth making, and second, because of our recognition that if we cannot show that the evidence on which it is based is adequate to sustain it, then that evidence (or evidence of that sort) could *never* sustain *any* claim to know about the objective world. Thus, the claim that the epistemologist introduces can be made to look like an intelligible claim: it is motivated, in the context, by a general doubt concerning the warrantedness of our attitude of commitment to the mass of judgements that normally form the stopping point for all our justifications of our ordinary claims to know. Moreover, the claim is serving merely as a focus for the investigation of our right to our conviction that we know the judgements of the frame. If it cannot be shown that this implicit claim to knowledge is, at least in the most favourable sort of case, well-grounded, then this would constitute an objection to our holding on to the framework judgements, and to our basing any further knowledge claims on them. Viewing the sceptical argument this way, it seems to me that Cavell's objection to the second horn of his alleged dilemma is quite unable to get off the ground.

This suggestion for how the traditional epistemologist might defend himself against Cavell concedes the very special nature of the epistemologist's enquiry and it clearly assumes that the contemplative position, or more specifically the suspension of our ordinary attitude of commitment to common-sense, that marks the beginning of the sceptic's reflections, is itself intelligible. The assumption, plainly, is equivalent to a belief that philosophy is possible, that is, that there is a legitimate form of enquiry that does not arise within the confines of the common-sense attitude but addresses itself to that attitude itself and attempts to reveal its nature. The traditional consequence of this form of enquiry has, of course, been scepticism. The extra-common-sense perspective appears to show that at the limit of common sense lie knowledge claims which cannot be justified and to which, strictly, we have no right. Our ordinary attitude of commitment to the judgements that form the framework of our pratice appears to be revealed as presumptuous and dogmatic. I do not, of course, believe that this constitutes a satisfactory philosophical outcome; the tension between our philosophical assessment and our ordinary, unshakeable conviction is intolerable. However, it seems to me that the only philosophical response that holds any promise of a real resolution of this tension is one that sets out to provide a non-sceptical understanding of the lack of justification to the limit. We require an account of the conviction in the judgements of the frame that allows us to see why the lack of justification for these judgements does not render that conviction dogmatic; we need to see why the lack of justification at the limit does not constitute, to use an expression of Cavell's, 'a failure on our part'.

Cavell's rebuttal of the sceptic appears to set out to provide the account I have claimed we should be seeking. That is, it appears to attempt to provide an understanding of why the absence of justification at the limit is not a lack on our part, or rather of why our sense, while doing philosophy, that there is a claim that we need to justify is quite wrong. However, the unsatisfactoriness of the response lies in the fact that Cavell's demonstration of the lack of any need to address ourselves to the claim the epistemologist introduces, and provide the justification he wants, is given only from *within* the perspective (or confines) of our common-sense attitude. Starting from the perspective of common-sense engagement, all that Cavell really demonstrates is that from within common sense we do not feel the need either to assert or to justify the judgements which are our common property and which form, in part, the background to our practice, and that we would not, within common sense, find intelligible anyone who did feel such a need to assert or to justify these judgements. But none of this even addresses the question of our right to this attitude or to the ordinary convictions that lie behind it. The failure to provide a non-sceptical account of our conviction is transparent; the need to understand why we can 'feel content' with our lack of a sense of a need to justify (or assert) these background judgements has not even been acknowledged, let alone met.

In the end, therefore, Cavell's argument against the sceptic is philosophically unsatisfactory for the same reason that Moore's and Austin's arguments are. All three philosophers are using the complete unliveability of scepticism as a sufficient basis for criticizing the sceptic's reasoning. Our common-sense conviction is being taken by all three as a legitimate starting point from which to launch an attack on the assertions of the philosopher. Cavell does not, despite initial appearances to the contrary, avoid the dogmatism of Austin and Moore, but, like them, starts his criticisms of the sceptic's argument from the point at which our ordinary attitude towards the judgements and claims of ordinary practice has already been accepted as correct and warranted. All three philosophers share our ordinary conviction that we do not need to provide the justifications that the sceptic requires, but they do nothing towards providing an account of this conviction that reveals it as warranted and undogmatic; the conviction of the common sense is simply being used as the basis of a direct reply to the philosopher's argument. If there is a difference between them, it is only in that the dogmatism goes progressively deeper underground. In Moore, the dogmatic nature of the reply is entirely explicit; in Austin, it is a more or less implicit principle of his philosophical method; in Cavell, it assumes something more of the status of an unacknowledged entrenchment in our common-sense outlook. But whatever form the dogmatism takes, the objection to it is not merely that it is dogmatic, but that it precludes the sort of philosophical understanding of the nature of our ordinary conviction that is crucial to a satisfactory unravelling of the sceptical puzzle.

The only hope of a genuine resolution of scepticism must, therefore, begin by making our ordinary common-sense attitude a question for us. We must address ourselves directly to the question of the nature of the judgements that form the framework of our practice, and the nature of our commitment to them. For it seems plain that as long as we take our commitment at face value and interpret it as conviction concerning the truth of empirical propositions, then the sceptic will be able to make us feel that there is a need to justify these judgements, and our inability to provide the justification will continue to impress us as a failure on our part. It is precisely the unwillingness of Moore, Austin and Cavell to 'go further back' and question the nature of our commitment that makes it impossible for them to provide a philosophical understanding of why the sceptic is not a threat. The question we need to ask is: What could the status of these judgements, and the nature of our commitment to them, be such that our inability to justify them does not constitute a failure or lack on our part? It is, I am suggesting, only if we can provide a convincing answer to this question that the riddle of sceptism will be finally exposed and understood.

6

Wittgenstein on the Philosopher's Use of 'I Know'

I turn now to a discussion of Wittgenstein's remarks in *On Certainty* (hereafter OC). I want to argue that these remarks do point the way for an account of the status of the judgements that form the frame of our practice, and of our conviction concerning them, that reveals why the sceptic's assessment of these judgements as lacking a requisite justification, and of our conviction concerning them as presumptuous and dogmatic, is misguided or misconceived. Wittgenstein, like Moore, Austin and Cavell, accepts that any philosophically satisfactory response to the sceptic must yield an unqualified form of common sense. But Wittgenstein is also convinced that common sense itself cannot supply any sort of philosophical reply to the sceptic's argument; the philosopher cannot use the conviction of common sense as a basis for a direct reply to the sceptic, without sounding absurd and dogmatic. The complete unliveability of the sceptic's conclusion should not constitute the unexamined starting point of a rebuttal, but should present itself as something needing to be understood. Thus, the unliveability of scepticism must become the major focus of our question: How can our complete lack of doubt concerning the judgements of the frame be understood in such a way that it no longer appears, from a philosophical perspective, as presumptuous or hasty or dogmatic? Wittgenstein wants an understanding of our practice that both secures us our conviction and shows why we never needed the justifications that the sceptic believes are essential; that is, he wants an account of ordinary practice that is at once non-sceptical and undogmatic.

One of the most striking features of OC, and one by which Cavell would appear to have been influenced, is that Wittgenstein's remarks focus on the *examples* of propositions that the sceptic tries to doubt and Moore claims to know for certain. I shall label these propositions *Moore-type propositions*. I have claimed throughout this book that we should see the sceptic's reflections as, first of all, drawing our attention to the mass of judgements that form the frame of our practice, and secondly, as arguing that we cannot provide these implicit claims with the (apparently) requisite grounding. Wittgenstein, I want to suggest, regards Moore-type propositions as constituting these vital framework judgemnets. It is the role or status of these judgements that Wittgenstein wishes to examine. However, he clearly believes, on the one hand, that it is impossible to pick out these judgements by means of any identifying characteristic, and on the other, that there is no very clear boundary between judgements belonging to this special class and ordinary empirical propositions. Thus, he remarks:

> There . . . are certain types of case in which I rightly say I cannot be making a mistake, and Moore has given a few examples of such cases.
> I can enumerate various typical cases, but not give any common characteristic. (OC, 674)

> There are cases where doubt is unreasonable, but others where it seems logically impossible. And there seems to be no clear boundary between them. (OC, 454)

> It might be imagined that some propositions, of the form of empirical propositions, were hardened and functioned as channels for such empirical propositions as were not hardened but fluid; and that this relation altered with time, in that the fluid propositions hardened, and hard ones became fluid. (OC, 96)

Some of the examples of Moore-type propositions that crop up in the course of the book include the following: 'My name is

L W', 'The world existed for a long time before my birth', 'Everyone has parents', 'Everyone has a brain inside his skull', 'I have two hands', 'That's a tree', 'I am in England', 'I have never been on the Moon', 'I have never been to China', 'Water boils at 100°C', 'I know that the water in the kettle on the gas-flame will not freeze but boil', 'I am a human being', 'I flew from America to England a few days ago', 'I am sitting writing at the table'. It is clear from these examples that the class is very much a motley, including both the most familiar facts of science and common sense as well as propositions describing the speaker's own particular history and immediate surroundings. It is also clear that none of them has any claim to a special epistemic status; they do not, for instance, concern items of immediate awareness. However, Wittgenstein believes that they are all propositions which, in a normal context, would either not, without special reason, be remarked, or, if they were remarked, would not, without special reason, be doubted or questioned. Plainly, the best that we can do is offer a very rough characterization of what would constitute the class of Moore-type propositions at a given time and in a specific context. Thus, the class of Moore-type propositions might be thought of as the mass of both spoken and unspoken judgements which form, in the context, the completely unquestioned background against which all enquiry, description of the world, confirmation and disconfirmation of belief, etc., goes on; they are all the judgements that are either 'flamingly obvious' or which may be spoken with authority, which will be accepted without doubt, and which may be taken for granted in the justifications that we give for the knowledge claims or more interesting judgements that we advance.

Wittgenstein believes that it is only philosophers who, from their contemplative position, cut off from ordinary practice, feel the need to introduce knowledge claims concerning Moore-type propositions. Furthermore, he believes that having introduced such claims, the philosopher then finds it impossible either to state how he knows these propositions, or to establish that he does not know them at all. Yet it is certainly not acceptable to attempt to establish a claim of this sort simply by insisting, as Moore does, that one really does know it. For, as

Wittgenstein puts it, 'what reply does one make to someone who says "I believe it merely strikes you as if you know it"?' (OC, 489); 'That he does know it remains to be shown' (OC, 14); and 'Giving the assurance "I know" doesn't suffice' (OC, 15). Thus the philosopher's introduction of a knowledge claim concerning Moore-type propositions has the effect of making our commitment to them appear suddenly 'unjustified and presumptuous' (OC, 553). Wittgenstein sums up the point as follows:

> When one hears Moore say 'I *know* that that's a tree', one suddenly understands those who think that that has by no means been settled.
>
> The matter strikes one all at once as being unclear and blurred. It is as if Moore had put it in the wrong light.
>
> It is as if I were to see a painting (say a painted stage-set) and recognize what it represents from a long way off at once and without the slightest doubt. But now I step nearer: and then I see a lot of patches of different colour, which are all highly ambiguous and do not provide any certainty whatever. (OC, 481)
>
> It is as if 'I know' did not tolerate a metaphysical emphasis. (OC, 482)

The primary aim of OC, therefore, is to avoid the mistake of 'countering the assertion that one cannot know that [that's a tree], by saying "I do know it"' (OC, 521), and to steer a course between the sceptic's doubt and Moore's dogmatism. The unsatisfactoriness of both scepticism and Moore's response to it reveals, Wittgenstein believes, that our relationship to Moore-type propositions cannot properly be described in either positive or negative *epistemic* terms; our relationship to the propositions that form the background to all normal enquiry must be understood in some entirely different way. Furthermore, Wittgenstein does not rely merely on the philosophical unacceptability of both sceptical doubt and Moorean dogmatism to persuade us that our relationship to Moore-type propositions cannot properly be conceived as an epistemic one. One major strand of OC is a quite explicit attempt to show us that there are 'grammatical' objections to embedding Moore-type propositions in epistemic contexts (i.e. to placing them within the scope of expressions like 'I know that . . .', 'I doubt that . . .', etc.). However, the great interest of Wittgenstein's remarks lies in the fact that his reply, unlike Cavell's, does not consist solely in an attempt to show that we do not really understand the knowledge claims that the epistemologist introduces, or that there is no intelligible claim for us to consider, and that we therefore have no need to address ourselves to the task of providing the justifications that the sceptic seeks. Rather, Wittgenstein goes on to provide an account of our relationship to Moore-type propositions that allows us to see precisely why these propositions do not embed in epistemic contexts, and why the question of our justification for accepting or affirming them does not arise. Thus, it is the account of our relationship to Moore-type propositions in non-epistemic terms that yields the crucial understanding of the judgements that form the frame of our practice, and of our conviction concerning them, that is at once non-sceptical and undogmatic; it is this account, if it is successful, that exposes the riddle of scepticism by offering an alternative understanding of the nature of ordinary practice.

I shall, however, begin my discussion of Wittgenstein by setting out the main points by means of which he tries to persuade us that it is a misuse of the words 'I know' to say, in the sort of context in which the philosopher says it, 'I know that this is a hand'. These points are, of course, interesting in themselves, but for our purposes their importance lies chiefly in the fact that they bring out the unsatisfactoriness of attempting to conceive of our relationship to Moore-type propositions as an epistemic one. Our relationship to these judgements emerges as lacking a sort of distance that is essential to the coherent application of epistemic concepts like knowledge, belief, or doubt. This in turn serves to prepare the way for an account that illuminates the lack of distance between ourselves and Moore-type propositions, by showing that our relationship to them is not an epistemic one at all. The alternative account of our relationship to them will be developed in chapters 7 and 8.

Wittgenstein makes *four* criticisms of the traditional epistemologist's claim, 'I know that this is a hand'. All four criticisms involve the suggestion that there is an implication carried by the use of the words 'I know' that cannot be met by claims involving Moore-type propositions. It seems clear, however, that the sceptic's response to the criticisms would not be the same in all four cases. The first criticism pinpoints an implication that the sceptic would certainly agree is not met by his use of the words 'I know', but which he would argue is not constitutive of the legitimate employment of these words. The remaining three criticisms pinpoint implications that the sceptic might well accept are carried by the use of the words 'I know', but which he would also argue are met by claims involving Moore- type propositions. I shall discuss these counter-arguments of the sceptic in the course of setting out the four criticisms below. I shall save what I believe Moore's response to Wittgenstein's criticisms would be until the end of my discussion.

The first criticism I want to discuss is the one that Cavell makes so much of, namely, that is a feature of our ordinary language-game that when we make a knowledge claim we thereby represent ourselves as believing, or generally imply, that we are in possession of a piece of information that our audience does not have access to, either through lack of relevant evidence, or through lack of relevant expertise. The suggestion is that this implication is a condition of the intelligible assertion of a proposition of the form 'I know p' or, in a case where the claim to know is left implicit, of 'p'. In a case where this implication is not met, then a speaker who utters the words 'I know p' or 'p', with the apparent intention of providing his audience with evidence-based information or expert knowledge, fails to assert anything (make a move in the language-game) at all. Thus, the whole point of our ordinary language-game is held to be lost in a case where the proposition the speaker asserts or explicitly claims to know is either utterly common property, or is something we would normally accept without question. i.e. something for which the question of evidence or expertise would not normally arise; we simply could not make sense of someone who earnestly attempts to represent himself as knowing something that we, or he, could not possibly fail to be aware of. The point is made as follows:

> Someone says irrelevantly 'That's a tree'. He might say this sentence because he remembers having heard it in a similar situation; or he was suddenly struck by the tree's beauty and the sentence was an exclamation; or he was pronouncing the sentence to himself as a grammatical example; etc., etc. And now I ask him 'How did you mean that?' and he replies 'It was a piece of information directed at you'. Shouldn't I be at liberty to assume that he doesn't know what he is saying, if he is insane enough to want to give me this information? (OC, 468)

It is not, of course, that Wittegenstein wishes to claim that the sentences 'This is a hand' and 'I know that this is a hand', or knowledge claims (implicit or explicit) involving Moore-type propositions in general, are senseless, that such claims could never have a legitimate employment within our ordinary language-game. Rather, 'for each of these sentences I can imagine circumstances that turn it into a move in one of our language-games' (OC, 622). However, the claim the philosopher considers is, as Cavell is so careful to emphasize, always intended both as a serious claim to know, and to concern a judgement that would, in the context, represent part of the common property of competent speakers, and for which the implication that one is genuinely informing one's audience of something is precisely, and essentially, not met. Thus, 'the truths which Moore says he knows, are such as, roughly speaking, all of us knows, if he knows them' (OC,100). Our belief, while doing philosophy, that we understand Moore's knowledge claims derives, Wittgenstein suggests, from the fact that we can imagine these very same sentences being employed in circumstances that make their assertion intelligible:

I know there is a sick man lying here? Nonsense! I am
sitting at his bedside, I am looking attentively at his face. –
So I don't know it, then, that there is a sick man lying here?
Neither the question nor the assertion makes sense. Any
more than the assertion 'I am here', which I might yet use
at any moment, if suitable occasion presented itself . . . And 'I know that there's a sick man lying here',
used in an *unsuitable* situation, seems not to be nonsense
but rather seems matter-of-course, only because one can
fairly easily imagine a situation to fit it. (OC,10)

The sceptic would, of course, agree that the knowledge claim
that he investigates is one which, in the circumstances, could
not be used to convey genuine information to his audience.
However, he would also insist that this does not render his
introduction of the claim 'I know that this is a hand' unintelligible, or involve him in a misuse of the words 'I know'. The
sceptic would, on the one hand, argue that the implication that
one is saying something that could, in the context, be genuinely
informative is one that can be cancelled without any misuse of
the language. On the other hand, he could point out that his
philosophical reflections have led him to the apparent discovery that our ordinary practice rests on our implicitly
assuming that we know Moore-type propositions to be true and
that this serves to motivate and render intelligible his interest
in such normally pointless (because uninformative) knowledge
claims. It was for this reason that I argued that Cavell's attempt
to press this particular objection into a refutation of the sceptic
cannot succeed.

However, it seems to me that, given the overall form of
Wittgenstein's response to scepticism, he has no need to make
the current objection bear the amount of weight that Cavell
tries to place on it. Thus, it seems enough for Wittgenstein's
purpose that he establish merely that the traditional epistemologist's use of the words 'I know' is odd, at least to the extent
that his use of them cannot serve the point that our use of these
words ordinarily serves. For this on its own is already enough
partially to motivate an account which illuminates this pecu-
liarity, by showing that our relationship to Moore-type prop-

ositions is not an epistemic one. On the other hand, the fact that Moore-type propositions cannot be the object of knowledge claims serves to emphasize their role as framework to our practice. Thus, Moore-type propositions represent a type of judgement which either we all make automatically, simply in virtue of being participants in the practice, or which will be affirmed and accepted without question, in cases where the relevant portion of the framework is something that we do not yet share.'This is a hand', 'The world existed for a long time before my birth', 'Everyone has two parents' are, for those who are masters of the practice, Moore-type propositions of the first type; 'My name is M. McG', 'I have never been to China', 'I flew from America to England a few days ago' are Moore-type propositions of the second type. Again, all this serves partially to motivate an account that reveals why we all share these judgements or accept them without question, as a matter of course.

The second criticism that Wittgenstein makes of the traditional epistemologist's use of the words 'I know' concerns the connection between knowing and having grounds. Our use of the expression 'I know' is, he claims, connected 'in grammar' with the possibility of saying *how* we know, and hence with the possibility of stating the *grounds* on the basis of which our claim to know is made. Thus, 'one-says "I know" when one is ready to give compelling grounds. "I know" relates to the possibility of demonstrating the truth' (OC, 243). The sceptic would, of course, agree with this, for the whole force of his argument depends on its being a grammatical point that whether one knows is something that must be established. It is because saying 'I know' makes the question 'How do you know?' immediately legitimate that the sceptic can, first of all, demand grounds for the claim 'I know that this is a hand', and then go on to show that any grounds that can be offered in support of it are quite inadequate. What Wittgenstein wishes to suggest, on the other hand, is that the notion of grounds and grounding cannot be intelligibly applied to Moore-type propositions, and that this rules out, as a matter of grammar, the possibility of legitimately embedding these propositions in epistemic contexts.

Wittgenstein points out that, prior to undertaking his enquiry, the traditional epistemologist did not so much as connect
the idea of grounds with Moore-type propositions. 'We don't,
for example, arrive at [these propositions] as a result of
investigation' (OC, 138), 'we affirm them without special
testing' (OC, 136), they 'form the inherited background
against which [we] distinguish between true and false' (OC, 94).
But again, this is something that the sceptic would presumably
accept; and for him it serves only to bring out the unacceptable
presumptuousness of his former ways of proceeding. The
sceptic is quite happy to accept that we do not *normally* ask for
grounds here, and to argue that his philosophical reflections
make him realize, what he had not noticed before, that we
simply assume knowledge of these propositions and that we
need now to supply the grounds of our assumption. The main
thrust of Wittgenstein's remarks, therefore, is to persuade us
that we cannot actually understand the sceptic's attempt to
extend the notion of grounds to Moore-type proposition.

Our notion of giving grounds for a particular judgement is
primarily an idea of appealing to something that is both
independent of, and more certain than, the original judgement, and which provides good reason for supposing that the
original judgement is true. It is this that leads the traditional
epistemologist, first, to search for beliefs that are epistemologically prior to judgements about the objective world, and,
second, to construct a notion of experience, conceived purely
subjectively, that could serve as the apparently vital, independent evidential base. However, Wittgenstein is suggesting that
there is a difficulty in treating Moore-type propositions as
propositions that are in need, or are capable, of being
grounded; namely, that we could not possibly be more certain
of any proposition than we are already about these. Thus, we
cannot understand what it would be to ground these propositions in so far as they already represent the limit to certainty;
nothing could be more certain than they are and therfore
nothing could, grammatically, serve as grounds. With these
propositions, Wittgenstein believes, we have already 'arrived at
the rock bottom of [our] convictions' (OC, 248). He expresses
the point more fully as follows:

So if I say 'I know that I have two hands', and that is not supposed to express just my subjective certainty, I must be able to satisfy myself that I am right. But I can't do that, for my having two hands is not less certain before I have looked at them than afterwards. (OC, 245)

My having two hands is, in normal circumstances, as certain as anything that I could produce in evidence for it.
   That is why I am not in a position to take the sight of my two hands as evidence for it. (OC, 250)

Wittgenstein does not, of course, intend to use our absolute certainty concerning Moore-type propositions to establish that they cannot possibly be false, or that we certainly *know* them to be true. For 'from its *seeming* to me – to everyone – to be so, it doesn't follow that it *is* so' (OC, 2). The trouble with Moore's response to the sceptic is that it tries to use his own state of conviction as a ground for establishing an objective knowledge claim. One of Wittgenstein's main points is that we cannot, without looking unacceptably dogmatic, interpret the certainty that represents 'the rock bottom of [our] convictions' as certain knowledge of objective truths. The logical difficulty in asking for grounds in the case of Moore-type propositions is rather to be seen as showing that we cannot regard our certainty concerning them as a form of knowledge at all. 'One says "I know" when one is ready to give compelling grounds. "I know" relates to the possibility of demonstrating the truth . . . But if what [we] believe is of such a kind that the grounds [we] can give are no surer than [our] assertion, then we cannot say that [we] know what [we] believe' (OC, 243). The sceptic wanted to see our inability to ground Moore-type propositions, and hence to justify a claim to know them, as an *empirical* failing that must be remedied if our acceptance or affirmation of them is to be undogmatic. Wittgenstein wants to see our inability as a logical feature of our relationship to these propositions and not as a failing at all. Plainly, it is in the end the account that Wittgenstein offers of how our certainty can be construed non-epistemically that must convince us of whether he or the sceptic is right.

The third implication of our ordinary use of the words 'I know', which Wittgenstein believes cannot be met in the case of Moore-type propositions, relates to our ability to regard the embedded proposition as an hypothesis, as something which requires support and which may be doubted. That this is an implication of our ordinary use of 'I know' is, again, something that the sceptic's own argument depends on. Thus, the sceptic wants to regard it as an immediate consequence of expressing what was, for him, merely a presumption as an explicit knowledge claim – 'I know that this is a hand' – that the truth of the embedded proposition, or more generally, the world-view it represents, should now become a question for us. Indeed, he wants in the end to persuade us that our conception of the world as an independent physical reality is merely one hypothesis among a number of equally well supported alternatives. It is a matter of no importance to the sceptic that we do not ordinarily regard our world view as an hypothesis, but as 'the matter-of-course foundation for [our] research' (OC, 167). For the sceptic, all that this indicates is the general presumptuousness of ordinary practice. As far as he is concerned, whatever our ordinary attitude, the notion of an hypothesis is easily extended to the conception of reality that ordinarily forms the background for all enquiry.

Against this, Wittgenstein attempts to persuade us of the total emptiness of the idea that our world view can be treated as an hypothesis. He points out that, although the sceptic *says* he doubts Moore-type propositions, or treats them as hypotheses needing to be established, all practical signs of doubt are completely lacking. The fact that we cannot even begin to say what it would be really (i.e. practically) to doubt our world view reveals our complete inability genuinely to distance ourselves from the judgements in which it is expressed. When the sceptic introduces the knowledge claim and undertakes his epistemic enquiry, he certainly intends to treat our world view as an hypothesis, as something that is open to doubt and in need of justification. However, his total inability to breathe life into his doubt shows that he never really succeeds in treating our world view as an hypothesis at all. Moreover, the complete unliveability of sceptical doubt shows not only that sceptical

doubt is not real doubt but also that our attitude of commitment to Moore-type propositions is not properly interpreted as
belief. We talk of believing a proposition in cases where we
understand what it would be to doubt it, or withhold assent
from it. In cases where withholding assent is not, practically
speaking, an intelligible option, talk of asent itself makes no
real sense. In cases where doubt is hollow, 'isn't *belief* hollow
too?' (OC, 312). The essential distance from propositions that
allows the concepts of doubt and belief, evidence and justification, to apply is simply lacking in the case of Moore-type
propositions. Thus, what the unliveability of sceptical doubt
primarily shows, Wittgenstein believes, is that our relationship
to Moore-type propositions, whatever it is, is not a state of
believing them on the basis of available evidence. Again, the
conclusion does not attempt to establish the truth of any
proposition, but merely invites an entirely new interpretation
of the certainty that characterizes our relationship to our view
of the world.

   Wittgenstein's final criticism of the traditional epistemologist's use of epistemic concepts concerns the inapplicability of
the concept of a *mistake* to Moore-type propositions. As we
ordinarily use the words 'I know', we generally imply that the
idea of our being mistaken about the truth of the embedded
proposition at least makes sense. Thus, we understand what
sort of evidence might make us revise our initial assessment of
the proposition, and motivate the concession that we were
wrong, that we thought we knew, but in fact did not know, that
the embedded proposition was true. 'I may be sure of something, but still know what test might convince me of error. I am
e.g. quite sure of the date of a battle, but if I should find a different date in a recognised work of history, I should alter my
opinion, and this would not mean I lost all faith in judging'
(OC, 66). Our ordinary notion of a mistake is, therefore, a
concept of possessing a false belief that 'can be fitted in with
what [is] known aright' (OC, 74). It does not contain any idea of
our, as it were, losing our footing completely, but is linked
rather with the ideas of revising beliefs and reinterpreting
evidence. What Wittgenstein argues is that none of this makes
sense in connection with Moore-type propositions; here *the idea*

*of going wrong is not an idea of being mistaken, but of something
entirely different.*

Once again, the sceptic would generally accept that the use of
epistemic concepts implies that the possibility of being mistaken makes sense. Thus, when he introduces the claim to
know that the object before him is a hand, he clearly intends to
extend the notion of our possibly being mistaken to the
propositions that express his world view. For him, our ordinary
failure to entertain any idea of possibly being mistaken with
respect to Moore-type propositions is simply an oversight on
our part. The fact that his extension of the concept of a mistake
to these propositions leads him to draw the conclusion that we
might be wrong about absolutely everything does not, he
believes, cast any doubt on his use of the concept but constitutes a discovery of the weakness of our epistemic position. The
sceptic then tries to give colour to this discovery, or to his use of
the concept of a mistake, by using the image of an evil genius
(mad scientist) who knows the real truth, and who is aware of
(responsible for) our own benighted position.

Wittgenstein is here in agreement with the sceptic in so far as
he believes that if the notion of our possibly being mistaken is
extended to Moore-type propositions, then this would have the
effect of putting every judgement that we make in doubt. If I
doubt the proposition 'This is a hand', in circumstances in
which it is functioning as a Moore-type proposition, then I can
have no reason not to doubt everything, for nothing is more
certain than this proposition. In the case of Moore-type
propositions 'a doubt would seem to drag everything with it
and plunge it into chaos' (OC, 613); 'the foundation of all
judging would be taken away' (OC, 614). But for Wittgenstein,
this serves to show only that the concept of a mistake has ceased
to apply. Clearly, we can have no idea what it would be to
establish that we are in error regarding a Moore-type proposition, for establishing anything in circumstances where every
judgement has been undermined is impossible. What, then, can
our grip on the notion of a mistake reside in? The sceptic's
appeal to the image of an evil genius is really no help at all, since
he would be just as much subject to sceptical arguments as we
are; the firm ground that the sceptic tries to use to make sense

of his application of the concept of a mistake can itself be made to shift and send us reeling once again. There is, therefore, no coherent notion of a stopping point, or firm judgement, once the sceptic begins to apply the concept of error to the judgements that ordinarily form the background of enquiry. The sceptic's use of the notion of a mistake requires the latter to function without the friction of a system of established judgements to work against. This is at best not our ordinary concept of a mistake – and at worst completely empty.

The idea that the concept of a mistake does not apply to Moore-type propositions is not, of course, to be interpreted epistemically; there is, for instance, no suggestion that someone cannot go wrong in connection with these propositions. 'I cannot be making a mistake about (them). But that does not mean that I am infallible about (them)' (OC, 425). 'In certain circumstances a man cannot make a *mistake* ('can' is here used logically, and the proposition does not mean that a man cannot say anything false in these circumstances)' (OC, 155). The claim is, rather, that falling into falsehood in connection with Moore-type propositions is never a question of a mistake, but is always a sign of something more fundamentally amiss, of a mental disturbance, or of a failure to understand the words that have been uttered. Thus, 'If Moore were to pronounce the opposite of those propositions which he declares to be certain, we should not just not share his opinion: we should regard him as demented' (OC, 155). 'If my friend were to imagine one day that he had been living for a long time past in such and such a place, etc., etc., I should not call this a *mistake*, but rather a mental disturbance, perhaps a transient one' (OC, 71). 'Not every false belief of this sort is a mistake' (OC, 72). 'If I make certain false statements, it becomes uncertain whether I understand them' (OC, 81).

Getting it right about Moore-type propositions, or accepting them without question as beyond doubt, is to be regarded, therefore, as a condition of participation in ordinary practice. 'In order to make a mistake, a man must already judge in conformity with mankind' (OC, 156). 'The truth of my statements is the test of my *understanding* of these statements' (OC, 80). Judging as others do in respect of these propositions is not, therefore, a matter of 'agreement in opinions', but of shared participation in the language-game, or linguistic practice, of the community; it 'is not agreement in opinions but in form of life' (*Philosophical Investigations* (hereafter PI), 241). Thus, the use of notions like 'assent', 'opinion', 'belief', etc. is inappropriate in the case of judgements involving Moore-type propositions, for these concepts always imply that the alternatives ('dissent' and 'disbelief') at least make sense. The inapplicability of the concept of a mistake to Moore-type propositions does not reveal that we know them certainly to be true, for this gives a quite incorrect (i.e. epistemic) characterization of our relationship to them. Rather, what it reveals is that our attitude of commitment to Moore-type propositions is somehow prerequisite. No refutation of the sceptic (i.e. no proof that we really do *know* these propositions) can be constructed on the basis of the point. All that is suggested is that a proper understanding of the nature of our certainty concerning Moore-type propositions must expose it as belonging to a category other than knowledge of empirical truths, and quite outside the range of the judgements that are open to question or refutation, or that stand in need of justifying. Wittgenstein points to the special, non-epistemic nature of this certainty as follows:

> I know that this is my foot. I could not accept any experience as proof to the contrary. – That may be an exclamation; but what *follows* from it? At least that I shall act with a certainty that knows no doubt, in accordence with my belief. (OC, 360)

> (And) I would like to regard this certainty, not as something akin to hastiness or superficiality, but as a form of life. (OC, 358)

The difficulty of extending the notions of grounding, hyphothesis and mistake to Moore-type propositions is, therefore, to be taken as revealing that our relationship to these judgements is non-epistemic or prior to knowledge. It is simply a misconception on the traditional epistemologist's part to think of our view of the world, as it is expressed in these propositions as an hyphothesis, put forward on the basis of evidence which might be misleading. Our view of the world is not to be seen in the same way as, say, our view of the cause of the Second World War. The sceptic, Wittgenstein believes, is quite wrong to think that our relationship to propositions and theories advanced within the framework of our practice could somehow serve as the model for our relationship to the propositions which constitute the frame. Our relationship to Moore-type propositions is more immediate, more profound and more inexorable than this epistemological model suggests. We are still a long way short of understanding what this relationship is or how it is to be conceived, but the purpose of the current objections to knowledge claims involving Moore-type propositions is to persuade us that the work needs to be done. What we need is an account that explains the above failures of implication, by describing our relationship to the propositions of the frame in something other than epistemic terms.

Looking at Moore now, he would, presumably, agree with the sceptic that the implication that one's knowledge claim is genuinely informative is not constitutive of the meaning of the words 'I know', and can be detached without misuse of the language. However, he would presumably agree with Wittgenstein, against the sceptic, that the idea of providing grounds for a knowledge claim involving Moore-type propositions is, because nothing could be more certain than they are, problematic; that we cannot regard these propositons as hypotheses open to serious doubt; and that we cannot understand what it would be to be in error concerning them. Yet Moore wishes to see these latter three points, not as objections to claiming to know Moore-type propositons or to regarding our relationship to them as an epistemic one, but rather as a sign of the peculiar security of knowledge claims involving them. Moore sees the problems in applying the notions of grounding, hypothesis and mistake to Moore-type propositions as a reflection of the fact that we simply see that we cannot possibly be wrong about them, that they are beyond all question true. Wittgenstein is aware, not only of how these points are at odds with what is ordinarily implied by our use of the words 'I know', but also of the fact that, once our relationship to Moore-type propositions has been conceived in epistemic terms, it appears unacceptably dogmatic to move from *our* inability to doubt, or to understand what it would be to be mistaken about them, to the conclusion that we certainly know them to be true. One of the things that the possibility of constructing sceptical arguments brings out is that knowledge claims involving the propositions that express our world view and form the frame of our practice are no more intrinsically certain than knowledge claims that are made within the frame and which are subject to confirmation and disconfirmation. On the other hand, our inability, when we occupy the engaged perspective, to make the extension of the concepts of grounding, hypothesis or mistake to Moore-type propositions is believed by Wittgenstein to reveal something of great importance about our relationship to the propositions of the frame.

Thus, Wittgenstein's disagreement with Moore is precisely over the question whether our certainty regarding Moore-type propositons is to be understood epistemically, as certain knowledge of objective truths, or non-epistemically. All that is objectionable in Moore springs, not from his certainty, nor from his unwillingness to give way in the face of sceptical arguments, but from his representation of his certainty as a case of knowledge. 'I want to say: my not having been on the moon is as sure a thing for me as any grounds that I could give for it. And isn't that what Moore wants to say, when he says he *knows* all these things? – But is his knowing it really what is in question, and not rather that some of these propositions must be solid for us?' (OC, 111-12). 'Instead of "I know . . . ", couldn't Moore have said "It stands fast for me that . . . "? And further: "It stands fast for me and many others . . . "' (OC, 116). 'I should like to say: Moore does not *know* what he asserts he knows, but it stands fast for him, as also for me; regarding it as absolutely solid is part of our *method* of doubt and enquiry' (OC, 151). '[I]t is not that on some points men know the truth with perfect certainty. No: perfect certainty is only a matter of their attitude' (OC, 404). 'What we have here is a foundation for all my action. But it seems to me that it is wrongly expressed by the words "I know"'(OC, 414).

Wittgenstein's own view, therefore, is that we should, on the one hand, recognize how very specialised the use of "I know" is (OC, 11). Our ordinary use of 'I know' is such that only knowledge claims meeting all four of the above implications are ever made; that is to say, its use is restricted to propositions that are advanced *within* the framework of judgements which together constitute our view of the world. On the other hand, he believes that we should see the limit on making clear sense of the above four implications in connection with Moore-type propositions as revealing that these propositions play a special role in our practice. Thus:

> When Moore says he *knows* such and such, he is really enumerating a lot of empirical propositions which we affirm without special testing; propositions, that is, which have a peculiar logical role in the system of our empirical propositions. (OC, 136).

> Even if the most trustworthy of men assures me that he *knows* things are thus and so, this by itself cannot satisfy me that he does know. Only that he believes he knows. That is why Moore's assurance that he knows . . . does not interest us. The propositions, however, which Moore retails as examples of such known truths are indeed interesting. Not because anyone knows their truth, or believes he knows them, but because they all have a *similar* role in the system of our empirical judgements. (OC, 137).

It is, as I have repeatedly emphasized, the provision of an account of this special role that is to yield the non-sceptical and undogmatic understanding of our conviction concerning the judgements that form the framework of our practice, and allow us to see through the riddle of scepticism. The role or status of the judgements of the frame is to be explained in such a way that we can see how our relationship to them can be immediate and non-epistemic. The account of these judgements is to show why the absence of justifications for them does not either pose a threat to our conviction or render it dogmatic. The conviction is to be revealed as having a non-epistemic base that renders the question of justification entirely out of place. Our relationship to these judgements is to be shown to possess a sort of immediacy that puts questions of evidence and justification out of play. In the final two chapters, I turn to a discussion of the account of our relationship to Moore-type propositions that I believe Wittgenstein provides.

7

Wittgenstein on Certainty

The four points discussed in the previous chapter, concerning the difficulties involved in understanding the ordinary implications of an epistemic claim when it embeds a Moore-type proposition, already serves to underline certain striking features of our relationship to these propositions. First of all, it has become still clearer that these propositions are something that we as a community either share or are willing to accept without question, hence our inability to offer them up as pieces of information that are open to doubt. Second, the idea that these propositions form the framework for ordinary practice has been given greater definition, through Wittgenstein's uncovering of the difficulties involved in attempting to treat them as hypotheses which need grounding and which might turn out to be false. In general, our whole practice depends on the fact that there is no epistemic distance between us and these propositions, that is, that they are judgements that we cannot discard or entertain serious doubts about. '"We are quite sure of it" does not mean just that every single person is certain of it, but that we belong to a community which is bound together by science and education' (OC 298). What we must do now is address ourselves directly to the question of the status, or role, of the propositions that belong to the frame. What we need is an account of these propositions and our relationship to them that allows us to see why our conviction that they are beyond doubt is not unacceptably dogmatic.

However, my approach to the problem of understanding the role of Moore-type propositions in our practice is not to be entirely direct. For there is another strand in OC that feeds into the strand I have already developed and unites with it in an account of the notion of the frame. This is the strand represented by the fairly frequent remarks about mathematics. The importance of this strand may be appreciated when we reflect on the way in which a peculiar sort of understanding of the status of mathematical propositions influences or informs the traditional epistemologist's conception of empirical knowledge.

I argued in chapter 1, that the traditional epistemologist, having construed our relationship to the judgements of the frame epistemically, is led to search for evidence that could ground our system of beliefs about the objective world. It is, of course, vital to the traditional epistemologist's conception of well-groundedness that the question of justification should not arise all over again for the beliefs that are alleged to be epistemologically prior to, and to serve as evidence for, our beliefs about the nature of reality. Thus, the beliefs that form the basis of our system of empirical beliefs must be such that we can know indubitably that they are true. Only then, it is argued, could the threatened regress of justification be halted, and only then could belief cease to be entirely arbitrary and become well-grounded. The ideal of indubitable, or intrinsically certain, belief that the traditional epistemologist operates with is generally supported by an appeal to the certainty that attaches to the propositions of logic and mathematics. Thus, it is generally supposed that our certainty concerning, say, $2 + 2 = 4$ or $-(p\& - p)$ should be understood as a state of mind in which we see that we cannot possibly be wrong. If no such beliefs can be found, then, the traditional epistemologist believes, all belief is arbitrary and knowledge is impossible. As we saw in chapter 1, the traditional epistemologist is led to construct a conception of experience, as something that can be conceived and described without reference to the objective world, which could provide the content for these epistemologically basic, indubitable beliefs. The intrinsic certainty of beliefs concerning experience, conceived in this purely subjective way, is held to reside in the fact that their content does not go beyond what is verified by the immediately given.

There are two crucial difficulties for the traditional conception of the basis of empirical knowledge. First of all, it has proved extremely difficult to defend the claim that beliefs about immediate experience meet the traditional epistemologist's own standard of intrinsic certainty. For, in order to derive a propositional belief from what is immediately given, what is given must be described in general terms. But describing the given in general terms immediately opens up a possibility of misjudgement, or at least of misunderstanding. The traditional epistemologist thus comes under pressure to reduce the content of the beliefs that form the foundation, until he ends up with beliefs that have no general content but are expressible, if they are expressible at all, only by 'This' plus a mental gesture. But now we are brought face to face with the second difficulty for the traditional conception of knowledge. For it seems clear that the minimal beliefs that the traditional epistemologist ends up with in his foundation are actually incapable of founding anything whatever. And even if we allow a richer conception of the content of beliefs about immediate experience, it still seems clear that, given that experience is being conceived in a purely subjective way, there is no hope of using these beliefs to eliminate the sceptical alternatives and justify our beliefs concerning the external world.

It seems, therefore, that while the traditional epistemologist regards the ideal of intrinsic certainty as essential if our system of empirical belief is ever to be shown to be well-grounded or non-arbitrary, the ideal itself serves ultimately to eliminate all hope of our ever justifying our beliefs concerning the objective world. Thus, what looks at first as if it will put an end to the threatened regress of justification and deliver us *from* the hands of the sceptic, ends by delivering us *into* the hands of the sceptic, at least as far as our beliefs about the external world are concerned. As long as we remain convinced that the only way to meet the sceptic's demand that we show our system of empirical beliefs to be well-grounded is to uncover indubitable beliefs that are epistemologically prior to our beliefs about the objective world, then we seem inevitably to find ourselves, either with an extremely confined set of beliefs, or with no justifiable beliefs at all.

In the light of all this, it should come as no surprise that

Wittgenstein's response to the sceptic – that is to say, his account of our relationship to Moore-type propositions – is underpinned in part by a reinterpretation of the certainty that attaches to the propositions of logic and mathematics. 'I want to say: If one doesn't marvel at the fact that the propositions of arithmetic (e.g. the multiplication tables) are "absolutely certain", then why should one be astonished that "This is my hand" is so equally?' (OC, 448). Wittgenstein's account of the role of Moore-type propositions in our practice is linked with an attempt to free us from a misconception of the certainty of the *a priori* sciences. He intends to replace the misconception of certainty as a state of mind in which we see that we cannot possibly be wrong, with an understanding that holds that the absolute security of the propositions of logic and mathematics resides, not in any special *epistemic* property that would make them knowable through the use of reason alone, but in the 'logical role' that these propositions play in our practice of inference and calculation. 'Knowledge in mathematics: Here one has to keep on reminding oneself of the unimportance of the "inner process" or "state" and ask "Why should it be important? What does it matter to me?" What is interesting is how we *use* mathematical propositions' (OC, 38). Given a new understanding of the security of the propositions of logic and mathematics, we shall then be in a position to understand how what appear to be empirical propositions (i.e. all the Moore-type propositions) could play exactly the same logical role *vis-à-vis* our practice of judging and describing.

The traditional epistemologist's understanding of the certainty of logic and mathematics depends crucially on the idea that mathematical and logical propositions have the status of *absolutely necessary truths*, that proofs and calculations follow up absolutely necessary links between propositions, and that human practice plays absolutely no role whatever in determining what the logical and mathematical truths are. Our certainty concerning the propositions of logic and mathematics is seen as a form of immediate intuition that the truths these propositions express could not, in any sense at all, be otherwise. Wittgenstein's reinterpretation of the certainty that attaches to mathematics and logic begins with an attack on the idea that the propositions of logic and mathematics constitute a body of truths generated by the absolutely necessary workings of a rigid calculus. The traditional conception of mathematics and logic tries to see our practice of inferring and calculating as underpinned by, or grounded in, a calculus that works inexorably to produce the absolutely necessary logical and mathematical truths. It is in this way that the tradition attempts to do justice to our sense that we have absolutely no choice where mathematics and logic are concerned, that they are entirely non- arbitrary, necessary and inexorable.

In the *Tractatus* (hereafter, TLP), Wittgenstein had also held to what might be called an 'objectivist' view of logical and mathematical truth. The isomorphism between language and reality and the strict independence of atomic propositions that the picture theory demanded, allowed Wittgenstein a peculiarly satisfying view of logical truth. The propositions of logic were both determined by and displayed the limits on possible worlds, by displaying the limits on possible structurally consistent sets of propositions. Logic puts the limits on possible structures of reality on show, and thereby reveals all that is absolutely unalterable in reality itself, namely its form. The nature of logic, in particular, its necessity and *a priority*, is therefore seen as having its foundation in reality itself. Logic is a sort of super-physics that tells us, or rather shows us not how reality happens to be but how it absolutely must be. It is not, of course that logic somehow *corresponds* with reality, for the propositions of logic do not *say* anything *about* reality – but logic and mathematics serve to reveal what the absolutely necessary or formal properties of reality are. Thus, we make absolutely no contribution as far as logic and mathematics are concerned; they are adamantine and absolute; they represent all that is essential and eternal.

The *Tractatus* account of logic and mathematics does not make use of the myth of a special realm of objects, but it does nevertheless regard logical and mathematical necessity as something absolutely hard and unalterable. This absolute hardness arises, not because of the peculiar nature of the facts that logical and mathematical necessity reflect, but because logic and mathematics represent the structural limit on the form that the facts can take. Logic and mathematics are not *about* anything but they still show us something that is objectively necessary. Thus:

> The exploration of logic means the exploration of *everything that is subject to law*. And outside logic everything is accidental. (TLP, 6.3)

> The only necessity that exists is logical necessity. (TLP, 6.37)

The Picture Theory of Meaning, which underpins the *Tractatus* account of logical necessity, is more or less completely rejected in the later philosophy, and the task of understanding the nature of logic and mathematics is begun all over again. In the later philosophy, Wittgenstein is still just as much against the idea that logic and mathematics constitute 'bodies of doctrine', but he is also now against the idea that they represent something adamantine and absolute and independent of us, a sort of super-physics. He believes that we have a natural inclination to suppose that q's following from $(p \supset q)$ & p in a logical proof represents an absolute necessity in the nature of things, or in the nature of propositions. We have an idea of the 'logical machine' that works inexorably to produce q given $(p \supset q)$ & p, and whose workings justify our procedures for drawing inferences. In the later philosophy, he set out to show us both the emptiness of this picture and the nature of the misunderstanding on which it is based.

Thus, he argues that when we write down, say, $\vdash (p \supset q)$ & $p \vdash q$, all we have done is write down a list of propositions. There is nothing corresponding to a link between the propositions $(p \supset q)$ & p and the proposition q, that already made q the correct and inevitable conclusion before it was even written down. He sets out the argument as follows:

> One is often in the dark about what following and inferring really consist in; what kind of fact, and what kind of process, it is. The peculiar use of these verbs suggests to us that following is the existence of a connexion between

propositions, which connexion we follow up when we infer. This comes out very instructively in Russell's account. That a proposition ⊢ q follows from a proposition ⊢ (p ⊃ q) & p is here a fundamental law of logic.

$$\vdash (p \supset q) \,\&\, p \vdash q$$

Now this, one says, justifies us in inferring ⊢ q from ⊢ (p ⊃ q) & p. But what does 'inferring', the procedure that is now justified, consist in? Surely in this: that in some language-game we utter, or write down (etc.), the one proposition as an assertion after the other; and how can the fundamental law justify me in *this*? (*Remarks On The Foundations Of Mathematics* (hereafter RFM), I, 19)

In his fundamental law Russell seems to be saying of a proposition: 'It already follows – all I still have to do is, to infer it'. Thus Frege somewhere says that the straight line which connects any two points is really already there before we draw it; and it is the same when we say that the transitions, say in the series +2, have already been made before we make them orally or in writing – as it were tracing them. (RFM, I, 21)

One might reply to someone who said this: Here you are using a picture . . . (I)f . . . the transitions which someone is to make on the order 'add 2' are so determined by training that we can predict with perfect certainty how he will go, even when he has never up to now taken *this* step – then it may be natural to us to use this picture of the situation: the steps are already taken and he is just writing them down. (RFM, I, 22)

Thus, Wittgenstein believes that the idea of an ethereal logical machine whose workings justify our practice is really no more than a picture. This is not, however, intended to constitute any sort of sceptical threat to our practice of inferring and deriving. It is not, for instance, intended to show that we are not *correct* when we derive ⊢ q from ⊢ (p ⊃ q) & p but only that there is nothing in independent reality that provides the foundation for this notion of what counts as correct inference. The idea is that our practice of inferring never needed the underpinning that the picture of the logical machine – of something absolute and essential in reality or in the calculus itself – tries to give it. Rather, this picture is an expression of one very important feature of our practice: that it is a practice in which we all share and in which we tolerate no deviations. An absolutely strict rigidity in what we count as valid inference or correct calculation is part of the 'grammar' of these language-games. Yet we perpetually attempt to project this feature of the language-game onto the world, so that the rigidity is thought to be in the the calculus itself, or in the 'logical structure of reality', which we know by intuition. The picture we construct really does no more than express our own commitment to counting nothing but this as logical inference, and our own feeling of 'going automatically' that our training has left us with. 'Now we talk of the 'inexorability' of logic; and think of the laws of logic as inexorable, still more inexorable than the laws of nature ... (I)t is *we* that are inexorable in applying these laws' (RFM, I, 118).

Wittgenstein suggests that we should abandon the idea that logic and mathematics form a system of true propositions, and think instead of logical and mathematical propositions as constituting, or defining, a system of *techniques*, which we employ in ordinary life whenever we move from one proposition to another in a logical inference of mathematical calculation. The techniques, like all the other techniques we employ, have grown up and developed in the course of the practical lives of human beings. The question whether the propositions themselves are true or false is, at bottom, entirely empty, for it overlooks their technique-constituting role. What matters is that these techniques have an established and vital role in our lives; calling then 'true' does not add anything to the fact of their being used, it is an honorific title which serves, if it serves any purpose at all, to show that these propositions are not put in question. Wittgenstein makes the point as follows:

> The steps which are not brought into question are logical inferences. But the reason is not that they 'certainly

correspond to the truth' – or something of the sort – no, it is just this that is called 'Thinking', 'speaking', 'inferring', 'arguing'. There is not any question at all here of some correspondence between what is said and reality; rather is logic *antecedent* to any such correspondence; in the same sense, that is, as that in which the establishment of a method of measurement is antecedent to the correctness or incorrectness of a statement of length. (RFM, I, 156)

In so far as the propositions of logic and mathematics are definitive of the techniques of thinking, inferring and calculating, all participation in our practice presupposes them: we cannot think, or infer, or calculate except by accepting and applying, in accordance with the practice, the propositions of logic and mathematics. Within the practice in which the propositions of logic and mathematics have this special role, arguments can be assessed for validity, calculations for correctness, and so on, but the techniques that are being employed cannot come up for assessment in the same way. The techniques *prove themselves*, and their worth is shown in the fact that they are used. Within our practice someone may infer or calculate correctly or incorrectly, but this does not mean in a way that conforms, or does not conform, with what 'the logical machine really does produce'. Rather, it means in conformity, or out of conformity, with our actual practice of calculating and drawing inferences. The conflict in incorrect inference or calculation is not between what is thought and objective facts but between the steps that have been made and our practice; the role that was formerly played by the empty notions of logical and mathematical reality is now played by the idea of the established practice.

Having taken the step of viewing mathematics and logic as constitutive of a system of techniques that are employed in our everyday lives, we can now cease to feel threatened by the emptiness of the picture of absolute necessities underpinning logic and mathematics. On the new account, it is enough that these are the techniques that have developed, that have their roots in human pre-history, and that are entrenched in a million different applications. These techniques do not stand in need of the sort of grounding that the traditional epistemologist's 'bad picture' seeks to give them; they are simply, along with certain other techniques, a peculiarly entrenched part of our natural human heritage. The necessity of these propositions is a reflection of the fact that they play a regulative role in the practice of inference and calculation. It is necessary that '4' comes after '3', '3' after '2', '2' after '1' in the natural number series, for only saying the numbers in this order qualifies as exercising the technique of counting; it is necessary that q follows from (p ⊃ q) & p for only this transition qualifies as exercising the technique of logical inference or rational thought. The propositions of logic and mathematics show what our techniques of inference and calculation are, and their necessity springs from the fact that *nothing else counts* as inference or calculation. Any sense that this makes the propositions of logic and mathematics arbitrary, subject to alteration by fiat, ought to have been removed by the emphasis on the way these techniques have emerged in the course of, and are deeply entrenched in, our practical lives: we can no more change them at will than we can cease to live in the way that our nature and our culture have made inevitable to us.

Wittgenstein sets out the point as follows:

'But then what does the peculiar inexorability of mathematics consist in?' – Would not the inexorability with which two follows one and three two be a good example? – But presumably this means: *follows in the series of cardinal numbers*; for in a different series something different follows. And isn't *this* series just *defined* by this sequence? – 'Is that supposed to mean that it is equally correct whichever way a person counts, and that anyone can count as he pleases?' – We should presumably not call it 'counting' if everyone said the numbers one after the other *anyhow*; but of course it is not simply a question of a name. For what we call 'counting' is an important part of our life's activities. Counting (and that means counting like *this*) is a technique that is employed daily in the most various operations of our lives. And that is why we learn to count as we do: with endless practice, with merciless exactitude; that is why it is inexorably insisted that we shall say 'two' after 'one', 'three' after 'two', and so on. – 'But is this counting only a *use*, then; isn't there also some truth corresponding to this sequence?' The *truth* is that counting has proved to pay. – 'Then do you want to say that 'being true' means: being usable (or useful)?' – No, not that; but that it can't be said of the series of natural numbers – any more than of our language – that it is true, but: that it is usable, and, above all, *it is used*. (RFM, I, 4)

The abstract systems of mathematics and logic, which might be presented in a text book, merely systematize, or set out in a way that is neutral between different applications, techniques that exist primarily as *applied* techniques, as modes of transition that we constantly employ in connection with concrete, empirical propositions in the course of our everyday lives. The pure disciplines are, as it were, grafted onto the living practice of applying techniques in calculation and inference. 'It is the use outside mathematics, and so the *meaning* of the signs, that makes the sign-game into mathematics' (RFM, V, 2). The pure disciplines do not in any sense provide a *foundation* for the applied practice; the 'foundation' of the practice lies entirely in the fact that it has woven itself indispensably into our lives. This perhaps explains Wittgenstein's notoriously hostile attitude towards any form of mathematical or logical revisionism, and his sometimes cavalier attitude towards the logical paradoxes. For Wittgenstein, '[t]here can't be any "leading problems" of mathematical logic, if these are supposed to be problems whose solution would at long last give us the right to do arithmetic as we do' (*Philosophical Grammar*, part II, section 12, p. 296).

The pure disciplines of mathematics and logic are not, of course, confined to a descriptive, systematizing role. New techniques for making transitions between propositions may be disclosed by means of pure mathematical and logical proofs. However, Wittgenstein believes that it is wrong to regard these proofs as uncovering, or allowing us to discover, essential properties or connections that were, in some sense, 'already there'. The idea that the following proof:

reveals it as an essential property of a rectangle, that it can be constructed from two parallelograms and two triangles, is best seen as a projection of our own sense of the significance of the pattern we have constructed (see RFM, I, 50). Thus we feel no temptation to regard the following:

as revealing an essential property of a rectangle, simply because the picture is not one that we can do anything with (RFM, I, 70). Proofs, Wittgenstein believes, construct patterns that we recognize we can use in countless ways. The pattern wasn't there prior to our construction of it, waiting to be revealed. We put it in the archives as, in this case, a further criterion of rectangularity: a rectangle is a figure that can be constructed in this (memorable and significant) way.

It is not, however, as Wittgenstein continually stresses, that we are, in the above proof, doing an *experiment* with a rectangle, or finding out what, as a matter of experience we can do with it. It is, for instance, very important that we could have come to exactly the same result simply by thinking about it; we do not have to take paper and scissors or ruler and pencil and physically divide the rectangle, as we would if we were discovering some contingent property of it, say that it is made of material thin enough to be cut by these rather blunt scissors. Furthermore, we show by our attitude towards the result of the proof that we are not performing an experiment, for we do not take ourselves to have established a property of rectangles that could change or decay, or which some exceptional rectangles may lack. We have not made a discovery concerning rectangles at all but have, rather, extended and enriched our concept of a rectangle. In general, the propositions of logic and mathematics can be known with certainty *a priori* because they constitute the criteria by means of which we judge whether a mathematical calculation or a logical inference is correct. The propositions of logic and mathematics define everything that is essential in our practice of inference and calculation.

On Wittgenstein's view of mathematics and logic, our all inferring and calculation in the same way is not to be explained by the spurious idea of a common intuition into the absolutely necessary workings of a rigid calculus. Rather, our mutual participation in the practice of inferring and calculating is to be seen as a result of our shared natural propensity to respond to the training that we receive in techniques for making transitions between propositions in the very same way. As a result of our training in techniques of inference and calculation we come to have a point of view that makes these particular further applications of the techniques the ones that *must* be made. Our natural response to our training is to leave us with no sense of choice; drawing and acting on those inferences which conform to our general practice becomes part of our nature. From the point of view of someone who has been trained, the techniques of inference and calculation are something that he applies inexorably. There is no foundation for our techniques that could, from the point of view of a non-participant in our practice, *justify* the steps we take or the applications we make. But anyone who cannot be brought to respond as we do will be deemed mad or incompetent, incapable of acquiring an immensely important human skill.

We are now in a position to understand Wittgenstein's idea that our certainty concerning the propositions of mathematics and logic is pre-epistemic. It has been argued that these propositions are such that the question whether they are true or false is not appropriate, since they play the role of defining techniques of inference and calculation. Our certainty regarding them is, therefore, quite clearly not a case of being sure that certain things are so. Rather, our certainty reflects our mastery of the techniques of a practice in which we are participants; it is a form of practical confidence that is better expressed in the words 'This is what we do' than in the words 'This is true'. The certainty is to be seen as the birthright of every acculturated member of the community, who has learnt to calculate and how to think or infer. It is a certainty that is not to be justified propositionally, by a proof that the propositions one affirms are true, but by the successful exercise of the capacity to employ the techniques concerned. There is no question of whether an individual really knows these propositions to be true, but at most a practical question of whether he is to be regarded as a competent member of the practice. The latter question is finally settled by the individual's getting it right (doing what we all do) often enough. What counts as 'enough' here may vary with circumstances, but it is clear that there comes a point where the criteria for mastery are fulfilled and not to accredit the individual becomes absurdly over-scrupulous, and eventually a form of madness.

It is important to see that the final remark of the previous paragraph does not conceal a dogmatic rejection of the sceptic, equivalent to Moore's insistence that he really does know that this is a hand: I really can do sums. The crucial difference betwen the two cases arises out of a difference between criteria for knowledge and criteria for mastery of a practical skill, like the ability to count or add up. The original sceptical problem turns on the fact that the concept of knowledge incorporates, as a condition of being fulfilled, an objective condition: the world must be as one affirms it to be. When the philosopher uses the concept of knowledge in connection with Moore-type propositions, the logic of the concept requires that there should exist a distinction between its merely appearing to him that he knows and his actually knowing. What the philosopher then discovers is that anything that he can offer as independent evidence for his knowledge claim is quite unable to establish that he really does know; the power of deciding the matter has been taken out of his hands. However, when it comes to the criteria for mastery of a practical skill, the crucial distinction between appearance and reality cannot be made. Thus, once it has been established that an individual can perform the act of ϕing reliably, in a sufficient variety of circumstances, in conditions where elaborate hoaxes are ruled out, the question whether he is merely appearing to ϕ, but not really ϕing, does not make sense: appearing to ϕ is, in these circumstances, ϕing successfully. If a 'sceptic' still doubts whether the individual can ϕ, then the appropriate response is: 'Test him yourself', and the possibility of being satisfied is logically required.

The fact that the propositions of logic and mathematics have a technique-constituting role makes acceptance of these propositions a main criterion of mastery. It is not only that these propositions cannot come up for assessment in the same way that arguments and calculations made within the practice do, but that there is no room, within the practice, for anything but *certainty* regarding these propositions, anything else will count as failure to have mastered the techniques involved. Thus, mastery of the techniques of calculation and inference actually consists in part in the ability reliably to affirm the propositions that define those techniques. Saying 1, 2, 3, 5, 6, 7 . . . or $2 + 2 = 5$, is an indication that the speaker has not yet fully mastered the techniques of counting and adding; affirming $(p \supset q)$ & p and concluding $-q$ is an indication that one has not yet learnt how to reason. Hence: 'The *truth* of my statements is the test of my *understanding* of those statements' (OC, 80). 'That is to say: if I make certain false statements, it becomes uncertain whether I understand them' (OC, 81).

What has emerged, therefore, in this brief discussion of Wittgenstein's views on the philosophy of mathematics, is a new understanding, first, of why it makes no sense to doubt logical or mathematical propositions, and second, of the ground of our certainty concerning them. Wittgenstein has developed a conception of certainty that is unconnected with, and prior to, the idea of knowing. It is a notion of certainty that stands apart from the concept of justification, and to that extent it provides a model of what it is to be in a position to accept or affirm undogmatically a proposition that, in one sense, one has no grounds for. The next step is to look at Moore-type propositions and our conviction concerning them in the light of this new model. The question is whether we can extend the account of the status of logical and mathematical propositions, and of our relationship to them, to propositions which are, on the face of it, empirical propositions. Can proposition like 'This is a hand', 'The world has existed for a long time past', 'My name is M. McG', etc. be seen as playing a role in our practice that puts us in a position to accept or assert them authoritatively, without the question of justification or evidence ever arising? If we can, then we should indeed have been provided with the non-sceptical understanding of the absence of justification for the judgements of the frame for which we have been searching.

8

On the Status of Moore-Type Propositions

In the previous two chapters, I have outlined the two strands of *On Certainty* (OC) that prepare the way for a new account of the nature of our relationship to the judgements that form the framework of our practice. The sceptic is led to his assessment of these judgements as lacking a requisite justification because he construes our relationship to them as an epistemic relationship to empirical judgements. Wittgenstein's alternative account is to allow us to see our relationship to these judgements in such a way that the absence of justification for them no longer appears as presumptuous or dogmatic. The account is to allow us to understand what is wrong both with Moore's attempt to claim to know, and with the sceptic's attempt to doubt, Moore-type propositions, or the judgements of the frame. The two strands together are to show both why and how we are to conceive of our relationship to Moore-type propositions in entirely non-epistemic terms.

The first strand of OC, discussed in chapter 6 above, attempts to bring out the oddness of an epistemic claim involving Moore-type propositions, by showing that certain implications of our ordinary use of the words 'I know' either cannot be met or cannot be fully understood in the case of claims involving these judgements. I have suggested that we should not attempt to see this strand of OC as the whole of Wittgenstein's reply to the sceptic but should regard it as intended to motivate the idea that our relationship to these judgements is not an epistemic one. The failures of implication serve to reveal that these judgements have a special place in our practice. On the one hand, they constitute a system of judgements that we as a community either share or are willing to accept without question, and on the other, they constitute 'the rock bottom of [our] convictions', the unquestioned stopping point for all our enquiries and justifications of claims to know. None of this can be used as a basis for establishing knowledge claims involving Moore-type propositions, and Wittgenstein does not attempt to use these points in this way. Rather, these points are used as part of an overall argument that reveals the error of the sceptic's initial – and fatal – supposition that our relationship to Moore-type propositions is to be construed as an epistemic one.

The second strand of OC, discussed in chapter 7 above, is provided by Wittgenstein's reinterpretation of the nature of the certainty that attaches to the propositions of logic and mathematics. It is this strand that forms the real basis of the account of the nature of our relationship to the judgements of the frame. Wittgenstein's idea is that our certainty concerning the propositions of logic and mathematics is not a matter of immediate and infallible intuition into absolutely necessary truths, but a reflection of the logical or grammatical role that these propositions play *vis-à-vis* our practice of inference and calculation. Questions of truth and falsity, correctness and incorrectness, arise within our practice of inference and calculation, but they do not arise, in the same sense, at the level at which the techniques of inference and calculation are themselves constituted or defined. Thus, propositions that look *prima facie* as if they constitute a body of doctrine are seen by Wittgenstein as having the status of rules or regulative principles which constitute the techniques we employ in a million different contexts. Our certainty concerning them is nothing other than a reflection of our legitimate authority, as accredited participants in the practice, on what our techniques of inference and calculation are.

The importance of all this for thoughts about scepticism is, plainly, that it has provided a model for understanding certainty as a non-epistemic attitude to judgements that have a non-empirical role. Our certainty concerning the propositions of mathematics and logic has been shown to be prior to knowledge of the results of the application of logical and mathematical techniques in empricial contexts, and constitutive of our mastery of the techniques that we apply. It is a form of certainty for which the question of our justification for the judgements we accept is completely out of place; accepting these judgements amounts to nothing more than the exercise of an accreditied practical capacity. Furthermore, our participation in the practice of inferring and calculating has been shown to depend (gramatically) on these propositions holding fast for us; putting these propositions beyond question is a prerequisite for, or a criterion of, mastery of the techniques that we employ in our practice of inference and calculation. There can be no participation in the practice, i.e. no mastery, that at the same time either goes wrong about, or even puts in question, the propositions that define the techniques to be employed; getting these propositions right and treating them as beyond question is a criterion of our being able to calculate and reason. What we have to do now is see how this understanding applies to Moore-type propositions and our practice of describing the world in empirical judgements.

In the *Philosophical Investigations* (PI), Wittgenstein presents a problem for the idea that the meaning of a word consists in some sort of interpretation of it, in something that, as it were, comes before the mind when one grasps or understands it. The problem for this conception of meaning is presented in the form of a paradox. Thus, he argues that as long as we think of meaning as an interpretation (or of understanding as grasp of an interpretation), then since any interpretation can always be interpreted in indefinitely many ways, we shall be quite unable to make meaning (understanding) determinate, or to ground the notion of the correct use of a word. '"Whatever I do is, on some interpretation, in accord with (a) rule." – That is not what we ought to say, but rather: any interpretation still hangs in the air along with what it interprets, and cannot give it any support. Interpretations by themselves do not determine meaning' (PI, 198).

The difficulty is, therefore, that interpretations do not

indicate, or 'already contain', the applications that are to be made of them; interpretations must be applied. And however an interpretation is applied, the application can always be justified by some suitable interpretation of it. Thus, interpretations cannot provide the stopping point for the justification of the application of a word; they cannot show us how the word is to be applied, or ground the notions of correct and incorrect use of a word. We want, of course, to think of the meaning of a word as a *special* sort of interpretation, one that *cannot* be interpreted but which forges an inexorable link between that word and the use that is to be made of it. 'What one wants to say is: "Every sign is capable of interpretation, but the *meaning* mustn't be capable of interpretation. It is the last interpretation"' (*Blue Book*, p. 34). The development of the paradox that arises for this conception of meaning is a demonstration that this notion of a 'superlative interpretation' is empty: interpretations can *always* be variously interpreted.

The outcome of this discussion is the emergence of an entirely different conception of meaning and understanding. What the paradox arising from the conception of meaning as an interpretation 'shows us is that there is a way of grasping a rule which is *not* an *interpretation*, but which is exhibited in what we call "obeying the rule" and "going against it" in actual cases' (PI, 201). Thus, a link is made between the concept of meaning and the existence of a customary way of using an expression ('What we call "obeying the rule" and "going against it" in actual cases'). The meaning of an expression consists in the use that is customarily made of it within a practice. The normative notion of how an expression *ought* to be applied is, therefore, given its content by the existence of a practice of applying it. A given application of an expression (or rule) may conflict or conform, not with a use that is in some mysterious way already contained in a 'superlative interpretation', but with how the expression (or rule) is customarily used within a practice. Thus, 'a person goes by a sign-post only in so far as there exists a regular use of sign-posts, a custom' (PI, 198). 'To obey a rule, to make a report, to give an order, to play a game of chess, are *customs* (uses, institutions)' (PI, 199).

On this view of meaning, understanding a word is no longer

to be thought of as a matter of hitting on the 'correct' interpretation of it; it is not, except in rather special cases, a question of hitting on an interpretation of it at all. Rather, coming to understand an expression means coming to have the practical ability to use the expression in a way that conforms to the ordinary practice of employing it. Just as we are to think of the meaning of a word in terms of a customary technique for employing it, so we are to think of understanding a word as a practical mastery of that technique. 'To understand a language means to be master of a technique' (PI, 199). Understanding comes to be conceived, not as a state of knowing propositions (interpretations) but as a practical capacity. The criterion for possessing the capacity in question is, in part at least, that the individual speaker should actually be able to use the expression correctly, i.e. in conformity with the customary practice of employing it. Thus:

> But it is wrong to say: 'A child that has mastered a language-game must *know* certain things'?
> If instead of that one said 'must be *able to do* certain things' that would be a pleonasm, yet this is just what I want to counter the first sentence with. (OC, 534)

> The child, I should like to say, learns to react in such-and-such a way; and in so reacting it doesn't so far know anything. Knowing only begins at a later level. (OC, 538)

In this account of meaning and understanding, the practice of describing the world in language has come to be construed in much the same way that Wittgenstein, as we have already seen, construed the practice of calculating and inferring. Describing the world in language, like inferring or calculating, presupposes the existence of techniques, in this case, techniques of description. The techniques are determined by a system of judgements which members of the community either share, in virtue of being participants in the practice, or which they are prepared to accept on the authority of other speakers, without question or doubt. Taken as a whole this system of judgements establishes a practice of employing words to describe objects.

The system of judgements which together constitute our techniques for describing the world is thus playing a role, *vis-à-vis* our practice of describing, that is analogous to that which the propositions of logic and mathematics play *vis-à-vis* our practice of inference and calculation. Wittgenstein's idea, of course, is that the judgements that play this special role are those that are expressed by Moore-type propositions. Moore-type propositions are not context-free or universally shared in the way that the propositions of logic and mathematics are, but they are still, in the vital sense, propositions that are, in a given context, solid for us – they form a background which we either share automatically or which we are prepared to acquire without question. Thus, the propositions that Moore affirms – 'This is a hand', 'The world has existed for a long time past', 'I am a human being' – are held to play, in the context, the role of determining, or constituting, our techniques of empirical description. These propositions show how the words of our language are used; they show us what a 'hand' is, what 'the world' is, what a 'human being' is, and so on. 'When Moore says he *knows* such-and such, he is really enumerating a lot of empirical propositions which we affirm without special testing; propositions, that is, *which have a peculiar logical role in the system of our empirical propositions*' (OC, 136; my italics).

We are not, therefore, to think of Moore-type propositions as stating empirical truths, in the sense of something which has turned out to be so but which may have turned out otherwise. The judgements of the frame are not applying our language in propositions whose meaning is independent of their truth-value; for these judgements, their being true in part determines the meaning of the expressions being employed. Thus for these judgements 'the idea of "agreement with reality" does not have any clear application' (OC, 215). The technique-constituting role of these judgements requires that their 'truth' is a matter of course, or better, that these judgements are not put up for question. The purpose of Moore-type propositions is to show us (teach us), e.g., what a hand is, what a chair is, what colour red is, and so on. '"I know that that is a hand." And what is a hand? Well, *this* for example' (OC, 268). Clearly, doubting a judgement that shows what sort of thing it is that we are talking about deprives the words we utter of their meaning for it undermines the practice, or system of judgements, that constitutes their meaning. It is only by putting the judgement 'This is a hand' beyond doubt that we can succeed in making statements by means of the following 'I have a pain in this hand', 'I once broke this hand', 'This hand is weaker than the other', and so on. 'If I wanted to doubt whether this was my hand, how could I avoid doubting whether the word "hand" has any meaning?' (OC, 369). 'The fact that I use the word "hand" and all the other words in my sentence without a second thought, indeed that I should stand before the abyss if I wanted so much as to try doubting their meanings – shows that absence of doubt belongs to the essence of the language-game' (OC, 370).

In so far as Moore-type propositions play the role of fixing our empirical concepts, being certain about them becomes, of course, a criterion of linguistic mastery. In order to qualify, or be accredited, as a master of the language-game, a child must have 'taken on board' a mass of judgements that form the basis of our ability to describe the world in language, and must be prepared to accept others on the authority of speakers, without doubt or question. The only way to acquire the means to express a doubt about anything whatsoever is by accepting or being prepared to acknowledge the judgements that together serve to determine what our doubt means. 'Doubt comes after belief' (OC, 160). Learning how to judge or to describe the world, coming to be able to express an opinion about it, means first of all coming to share in the practice of judging, within which opinions may be advanced and defended. 'I must begin with not doubting: it is part of judging' (OC, 150). 'Moore does not *know* what he says he knows, but regarding it as solid is part of our *method* of enquiry' (OC, 151). 'In order to make a mistake [express and opinion, put forward an hypothesis, formulate a doubt, etc. (M. McG.)] a man must already judge in conformity with mankind' (OC, 156). 'If you are not certain of any fact, you cannot be certain of the meaning of your words' (OC, 114).

One important consequence of this account of the role of Moore-type propositions is that it allows us to interpret the certainty that individual speakers have concerning them in more or less the same way that we earlier understood our certainty concerning the propositions of mathematics and logic. Thus, my certainty regarding, say, the judgement 'This is a hand' is to be seen as a pre-epistemic attitude that is in part constitutive of my practical ability to speak the language. The judgement that this is a hand is not a piece of knowledge – a true, justified belief, based on evidence – but an authoritative expression of my established mastery of English. As in the case of our certainty concerning the propositions of logic and mathematics, my certainty concerning this judgement is best understood as having the form 'This is what we do'; it represents my practical mastery of the practice of speaking the language. It is not, therefore, a variety of certainty for which the question of justification arises. In general, we do not require evidence for how the words of our language are to be applied, but each of us, as masters of the language, can unselfconsciously and authoritatively show how the words of our language are used. If the question of expertise should be raised, then, as we have seen, it is always capable of being settled.

When the traditional epistemologist takes up his reflective stance on our practice, he has invariably taken our relation to our system of judgements to be a uniformly epistemic one. He believes that if any judgement in the system is to be justified, then we must be able to show that the judgements that normally form the framework and which, he believes, we are implicitly claiming to know, are well-grounded. It is, of course, by interpreting these framework judgements as implicit knowledge claims that the sceptic is able to make our practice as a whole look unacceptably presumptuous or dogmatic: we appear to be assuming that we know these judgements to be true, yet we are quite incapable of justifying our belief in them. Wittgenstein's idea is that this picture represents a misapprehension of the nature of the judgements that form the frame, and of our relationship to them. These judgements are not empirical propositions that we know or believe on the basis of evidence. Rather, they are constitutive of our descriptive techniques, and our acceptance or affirmation of them is the expression of our practical ability to use the language. At the bottom of our practice lies, not knowledge, but practical abilities to employ conceptual techniques. The idea of a foundation in certain knowledge is replaced by the idea of a basis in practical mastery of a system of judgements which together determine our techniques for describing the world in language.'[T]he end is not an ungrounded presupposition: it is an ungrounded way of acting' (OC, 110). 'Giving grounds . . . justifying the evidence, comes to an end; – but the end is not certain propositions striking us immediately as true, i.e. it is not a kind of *seeing* on our part; it is our *acting*, which lies at the bottom of the language-game' (OC, 204). '[I]t belongs to the logic of our scientific investigations that certain things are *in deed* not doubted' (OC, 342).

What Wittgenstein is offering us, therefore, is an alternative conception of human practice in the context of which our claims to know about the objective world are made. Our practice does not rest on knowledge, for which the question of justification can be made eternally to arise, but on practical mastery of descriptive techniques that is expressed in how we act, i.e. in the judgements we affirm (either explicitly or implicitly) in the course of our active, everyday lives. Our practical mastery of techniques of description is in an important sense primary, for without this mastery no moves can be made. It is 'the element in which arguments have their life' (OC, 105). The practice in which our mastery allows us to participate is to be conceived as a natural phenomenon, something that has emerged and evolved over the course of human history. The practice of employing descriptive techniques is something that we inherit through the training that constitutes our method of induction or acculturation. We must think of the practice itself as something that is established as a natural phenomenon in the world; it exists independently of any particular individual, but it is something in which we all participate. It is 'something that lies beyond being justified or unjustified; as it were, something animal' (OC, 359). '[I]t is not based on grounds. It is not reasonable (or unreasonable). It is there – like our life' (OC, 559).

I want to argue that this reassessment of what lies at the foundation of our practice provides an undogmatic unravelling of the sceptical problematic. It gives an account of the judgements of the frame that allows us to understand why the question of our justification for accepting or affirming them does not arise; it shows why the absence of justification for these judgements is not a lack. I believe that the account, unlike the treatment of scepticism offered by Moore, Austin and Cavell, does not merely defend the lack of justification for the judgements of the frame from *within* the entrenched outlook of common sense, which, by its very nature, cannot perceive the justifications that the sceptic seeks as necessary. Thus, we should see Wittgenstein as following the sceptic in the taking up of a reflective or philosophical attitude towards human practice, and then showing why the sceptic's assessment of the judgements of the frame as not well-grounded is based on a misconception of their nature. Wittgenstein's non-sceptical assessment of the lack of justification for the judgements of the frame reveals them as having a role that makes the question of establishing that they are true out of place. These judgements are absolutely secure, but not in the sense that they are 'intrinsically certain', as this is understood by the traditional epistemologist. Our conviction in them is not properly conceived as epistemic certainty regarding the truth of empirical propositions, for which the question of justification must inevitably arise, but as the immediate exercise of our practical mastery of our techniques for describing the world, for which the question of justification makes no sense.

However, I think there is probably a strong temptation at this point to think that there is a dogmatic rebuttal of scepticism underlying Wittgenstein's alleged unravelling of the sceptical problematic. It might be objected on behalf of the sceptic that in so far as Wittgenstein's account of human practice is given in a thoroughly naturalistic spirit, from within our ordinary outlook, there is inevitably a dogmatic rejection of scepticism implicit in it. Thus, in so far as the natural world of public objects, our awareness of these objects and our practice of using language to describe them, have all been taken for granted in the account, it might seem that all the vital questions have simply been begged against the sceptic. The failure to justify or legitimize the naturalistic outlook, which forms the backdrop for the account, may appear to amount to nothing better than a dogmatic entrenchment in our common-sense view, which leaves the problem of scepticism completely untouched, and which I earlier took to vitiate the replies of Moore, Austin and Cavell. Thus, while it may initially have been made to look as if Wittgenstein takes up an attitude of philosophical contemplation of ordinary practice, when we widen our focus we see that he has in fact transported the common-sense outlook entirely intact to his reflective position, and this has the effect of making his whole account rest on the dogmatic assumption that scepticism is false.

It is certainly true that nowhere in OC does Wittgenstein attempt to prove the reality of human practice. The outlook of the book, and I believe of Wittgenstein's later philosophy in general, is a thoroughgoing naturalism. The philosophical enterprise is conceived as the interrogation of a particular natural phenomenon – the phenomenon of human practice – in the attempt to understand its workings in such a way that philosophical puzzlement and perplexity no longer arises. The question is, clearly, whether a response to the sceptic that is grounded in this conception of philosophy is necessarily dogmatic. It can certainly be made to look as if it is. Thus, it can be made to seem that Wittgenstein, like Moore, is forced to admit that he 'has neither given nor attempted to give' the proof that the philosophical sceptic really needs, but rather that he has simply begged the question against the sceptic. And one is left wanting to say against Wittgenstein, as Wittgenstein at one point seems to say against Moore, that given the starting point, all the rest may be granted, but that the starting point itself simply assumes the falsity of the sceptic's assessment.

I want to argue that, tempting though all this seems, it is an entirely mistaken appraisal of the naturalism that forms the backdrop to Wittgenstein's account of the role of the judgements of the frame. To understand why it is mistaken, we need to look once again at the way in which scepticism arises within the philosophical context. I argued in chapter 1 that scepticism should not be identified simply with the familiar Sceptical Hypotheses that form the basis of the sceptic's objection to a representative knowledge claim involving a judgement of the frame. Rather, scepticism should be viewed as a complex phenomenon that begins with the taking up of a reflective or contemplative stance towards human practice. In his initial position, therefore, the sceptic should not be seen as holding a different attitude from someone who wishes to philosophize from the natural standpoint; if there is a difference, it would seem to lie in the absence of a commitment, on the sceptic's part, to preserving our ordinary outlook or conception of our relation to the objective world. This difference aside, the sceptic too begins by interrogating the phenomenon of human practice in order to achieve a reflective understanding of its workings; in particular, he wishes to discover which of the claims to know about the world that are advanced within it are well-grounded.

Having become thus reflective, the first thing that the sceptic observes about human practice is that it appears to operate within a framework of judgements which are either never remarked or, if they are remarked, are never questioned. In so far as we must, the sceptic believes, be taken to be making an implicit claim to know these judgements, then our right to affirm them would seem to depend on our being able to provide them with a satisfactory justification. The sceptic's next step is to claim that in order to justify these judgements we should have to show that the evidence on which they rest does in fact support them. It is at this point that the idea of evidence epistemologically prior to any judgements about the objective world – i.e. the idea of experience, conceived purely subjectively, as the basis of human knowledge – emerges. If human practice is to be well-grounded, we must be able to show that experience, conceived in this purely subjective manner, is a reliable guide to the nature of the objective world. What the sceptic appears to discover, of course, is that our alleged assumption of the reliability of sense experience cannot be discharged, and that all the judgements and claims of ordinary practice are to that extent defective. Having made this discovery, the sceptic is now obliged to admit that these claims and judgements ought to be suspended or withdrawn.

The sceptic's apparent discovery that human practice is not well-grounded leads, I believe, to a dual perplexity. The first source of perplexity, the one I have been discussing throughout this book, is that the sceptic is led to a philosophical assessment of ordinary practice that is completely at odds with the assessment that he necessarily makes when he takes up the engaged perspective of that practice once again. He has, from a philosophical perspective, shown to be a dogmatic or presumptuous judgements which, from another perspective, he cannot but feel to be entirely secure and quite without need of justification. However, there is a second source of perplexity, which I have not previously touched on: the sceptical conclusion concerning our right to make judgements about the nature of reality is in an important respect at odds with the position that the sceptic holds at the beginning of his philosophical enquiry. At the beginning of his enquiry the sceptic addresses himself to our practice of claiming to know things about objective reality, as a phenomenon that is to be investigated. The second source of perplexity lies in the fact that the conclusion he is led to draw concerning human practice has the effect of depriving him of the right to believe in the phenomenon he began by investigating.

On this view of the way scepticism arises, the sense of the sceptic's total isolation within experience, or, what comes to the same thing, of his total loss of the objective world, is something that comes only in the course of his inquiry, and is not there in it from the beginning. It is, I am suggesting, the sceptic's step of treating our framework judgements as empirical claims that must be established as true on the basis of independent evidence, that causes this problematic conception of experience to arise. However, once we recognize that the sceptic's solipsistic conception of experience is itself a product of what Wittgenstein believes to be a misapprehension of the nature of the judgements that form the frame of our practice, then we can see how an account which avoids this misapprehension has no need to address itself to the problems that this conception of experience gives rise to. An account which starts by taking up a reflective stance towards human practice but which is never led, as the sceptic is, either into holding that the judgements of the frame lack an essential justification, or into conjuring up the idea of experience as something conceivable purely subjectively, should not, therefore, be seen as begging any questions. The point is that such an account never allows the sceptic's

misapprehensions to arise and threaten either ordinary practice or the naturalistic outlook that characterizes our initial
position in philosophy. The natural outlook that is Wittgenstein's starting point should not, therefore, be regarded as
needing to regain ground from the sceptic: the sceptical
conclusion has not yet been allowed to arise and threaten it. It is
rather that if we follow the sceptic in his misapprehension of
the nature of ordinary practice, then the sceptical conclusion
inevitably arises within the contemplative position and swallows
up, not only common sense, but, more paradoxically, the
sceptic's own starting point as well. If the account of ordinary
practice that we achieve from the reflective perspective never
allows the sceptical misapprehension and consequent conclusion to arise, then *both ordinary practice and the naturalism of
the starting point remain entirely secure.*

The claim is, therefore, that the charge of dogmatism, on the
grounds of the naturalism that characterizes Wittgenstein's
reflective stance, is mistaken. Wittgenstien's rebuttal of the
sceptic remains importantly different from the replies of
Moore, Austin and Cavell. In the case of the latter three
philosophers, it is not merely that their enquiries are conducted
within a naturalistic attitude towards the phenomenon of
human practice. The arguments by means of which they block
the sceptical conclusion depend on the assumption that the
common-sense assessment of the judgements of the frame, as
certainly and beyond all question true, is the correct one. Thus,
it is only if we dogmatically reject the sceptic's assessment of the
judgements of the frame and accept them as true or 'flamingly
obvious', that Moore, Austin and Cavell can succeed in showing
that we have no need to hearken to the sceptic's doubts. And
this, I believe, is unacceptably dogmatic. Arguments which
start from the common-sense assessment of the judgements of
the frame necessarily fail to provide us with the means to resist
the sceptic's power, first of all, to persuade us to take up the reflective stance, and then to make us feel, from this perspective,
that the judgements of the frame require but cannot be given a
justification. Wittgenstein's response, by contrast, is not merely
a demonstration of the fact that from within our common-sense
perspective we feel no need to reply to the sceptic's doubts.

Wittgenstein's account of the role of the judgements of the frame, and of the nature of our certainty concerning them, provides a philosophical understanding that allows us to see why the question of our justification for accepting or affirming these judgements is out of place.

It is clear that this assessment of Wittgenstein's reply to the sceptic holds that there is an intimate link between our conception of the sceptical problematic and our capacity to see through or resolve it. I think it should come as no surprise that being clear about how to resolve the problematic should depend crucially on being clear about the precise way in which it arises. Yet I believe that the elusiveness of a satisfactory resolution has arisen in large part because philosophers have neglected precisely this point. The philosopher has generally attempted to grapple with scepticism at the point where the criticism of our system of judgements and knowledge claims has already begun, and has ignored the question of the nature of the reflective stance that constitutes the sceptic's initial position. The effect of this is that he has inevitably found himself in a position of attempting to recover lost ground. He is working to retrieve from the sceptic not only our ordinary judgements and assessments of knowledge claims but also our right to talk about the human community and its practice of judging and affirming claims to know about the world. If we have not first appreciated that scepticism is itself something that arises within an essentially naturalistic outlook, which it only later paradoxically undermines, then we shall wrongly conceive our task to be one not of preventing scepticism from arising but of regaining naturalism from the sceptic. In a sense, therefore, philosophers have not gone far enough back in their attempt to deal with the sceptic, and they are left trying to establish secure ground against the tide of his argument. The choice that inevitably presents itself at this point is, either to pull in our horns and accept idealist qualifications of our common-sense assertions, or to go dogmatic and simply reassert the outlook that scepticism appears to undermine.

It is, therefore, by paying attention to the preliminaries to the sceptical argument, in which the sceptic takes up his reflective attitude towards human practice, that we have been able to make out a case for holding that Wittgenstein's rebuttal of the sceptic is not question-begging. In so far as Wittgenstein provides an alternative assessment of the fact that we do not possess or require justifications for the judgements that form the frame of our practice, he prevents scepticism from arising, and we never find ourselves deprived of either the natural attitude or unqualified common sense. The crucial point is to recognize that Wittgenstein's account of the role of Moore-type propositions is to allow us to avoid ever losing ground to the sceptic. Thus, Wittgenstein's naturalism does not come in *after* the sceptical argument has been constructed, to show that our unshakeable conviction in the judgements of the frame makes the argument idle. Rather, the naturalism forms a backdrop to an account of the nature of our conviction and of the role of the judgements of the frame, that allows us to see why the absence of justification for these judgements is not a failure or lack.

We are, therefore, to think of Wittgenstein's account of the role of Moore-type propositions as an account of judgements that are made by human beings in the course of their active lives, within their natural environment. We need not, therefore, be anxious that Wittgenstein is leading us into a form of idealism, when he insists that nothing in what he says about Moore-type propositions is intended to establish that the view of the world that they express is certainly the correct one. It is clear that Wittgenstein is not attracted by a form of naturalism that attempts to argue that since our world view is the one that has evolved, it must certainly correspond with how things really are. But his alternative is not in any sense idealistic. Rather, the point is that we live in the natural world and, in the course of our active lives in it, we have developed tecniques for describing it. The question whether this system of techniques is true or false is simply grammatically out of place. 'I did not get my picture of the world by satisfying myself of its correctness. No: it is the inherited background against which I distinguish between true and false' (OC, 94). 'I have a world-picture. Is it true or false? Above all it is the substratum of all my enquiring and asserting' (OC, 162). 'If the true is what is grounded, then the ground is not *true*, nor yet false' (OC, 205). 'The ground' or 'the substratum' is the system of judgements that we make as a matter of course or are willing to accept unquestioned, and which together constitute our linguistic techniques. If someone does not accept the judgements that constitute our practice of employing words, then this is not a matter of doubting truths that we do not doubt, but of reacting to a training in the practice of describing the world in such a way that he can never acquire the ability to think or to use language. 'If someone asked us "but is that *true*?" we might say "yes" to him; and if he demanded grounds we might say "I can't give any grounds, but if you learn more you too will think the same". If this didn't come about, then he couldn't for example learn history' (OC, 206).

So far, my discussion has concentrated on Wittgenstein's idea that our certainty concerning Moore-type propositions should be construed along the lines of our certainty concerning logical and mathematical propositions; that is, as a practical certainty relating to how the expressions of our language are used, which is entirely independent of questions of justification. I have, therefore, talked rather glibly of Moore-type propositions 'playing the same role' *vis-à-vis* our practice of describing the world as, say, the propositions of arithmetic play *vis-à-vis* our practice of calculating. But can we really see propositions like 'This is a hand', 'My name is M. McG.', 'The world has existed for a long time past', etc. as on a par with propositions like '2 + 2 = 4'? That Wittgenstein regards the two as 'equally certain' is clear: 'The physical game is just as certain as the arithmetical' (OC, 447). 'We learn with the same inexorability that this is a chair as that 2 + 2 = 4' (OC, 455). 'We know with the same certainty with which we believe *any* mathematical proposition how the letters A and B are pronounced, what the colour of human blood is called, that other human beings have blood and call it "blood"' (OC, 340). Yet how are we to account for the fact that we have not (could not have) systematized Moore-type propositions 'in a logic book' (OC, 628)? That is, how are we to account for our own sense that there are important differences between the propositions that Wittgenstein gives as examples of Moore-type propositions and the propositions of mathematics and logic?

Wittgenstein's view of the role of the judgements of the frame requires that we should accept that, say, the proposition 'This is a hand', when it is functioning as a Moore-type proposition, is both necessary and *a priori*. It is necessary in somewhat the way in which 'This rod is one metre', said of the Metre Rod, is necessary. The concepts involved are not being applied to objects on the basis of evidence. Rather, the objects referred to are functioning as samples or standards; the objects serve to show us (or the child) what a metre, or what a hand, is. We, as it were, take hold of the object and use it to show what sort of thing it is that we call 'a hand' in our language. No question of justification for affirming the judgement arises. Those who are trained in the practice of using language are exhibiting their mastery in the attempt to train others in its techniques of description. The proposition is *a priori*, therefore, in the sense that the speaker's relation to the judgement he affirms is such that no question of his having made a mistake arises. The speaker is not asserting something that he believes on the basis of evidence, but exercising his practical capacity to employ the words of his language in the way he has been trained to, in accordance with the practice, i.e. correctly. Madness and misunderstandings may sometimes occur, but their occurrence does not, in perfectly unexceptional circumstances, provide a ground for doubting the competence of the current speaker. However, even if we are willing to accept all this, and hold that Moore-type propositions are necessary and *a priori* in the sense just described, there is still a feeling that 'This is a hand' *is* different from '2 + 2 = 4'.

Indeed, Wittgenstein seems willing to acknowledge that there is, in the end, a difference between Moore-type propositions and the propositions of logic and mathematics. At OC, 655-7 he writes:

> The mathematical proposition has, as it were, officially been given the stamp of incontestability. I.e.: 'Dispute about other things; *this* is immovable – it is a hinge on which our dispute can turn.'

> And one can *not* say that of the proposition that I am called L. W.

The propositions of mathematics might be said to be fossilised. – The proposition 'I am called . . . ' is not.

The proposition $2 + 2 = 4$ is, therefore, *never* open to question. Its status as a technique-constituting proposition is, as it were, universal: there are no circumstances, no matter how exceptional, in which it could make sense to treat it as something that needed to be established. Its status as a rule does not depend on the context or the speaker; it has, 'as it were officially, been given the stamp of incontestability'. The same, Wittgenstein is suggesting, does not hold for Moore-type propositions. In exceptional circumstances, 'My name is M. McG.', or 'I have two hands', may function as genuine empirical propositions, things about which I might conceivably be wrong, and which I may legitimately claim to know (or doubt). It is precisely this possibility that lent to the philosopher's knowledge claim whatever air of making sense it had. Yet this does not alter the fact that in normal circumstances, Moore-type propositions are incontrovertible, i.e. necessary and *a priori* in the sense described above. That is to say, for these, as for the propositions of logic and mathematics, the 'absence of doubt belongs to the essence of the language-game' (OC, 370). For 'if [we] want the door to turn, the hinges must stay put' (OC, 343).

The difference that exists between Moore-type propositions and the propositions of logic and mathematics does not, therefore, threaten Wittgenstein's basic insight that 'propositions of the form of empirical propositions, and not only propositions of logic, form the foundation of all operating with thoughts (with language)' (OC, 401). To doubt the 'empirical' propositions that are playing this role is as senseless as doubting the propositions of the multiplication table. It is like suggesting 'that a game has always been played wrong' (OC, 496). It is what is asserted within our practice that can be true or false. These notions do not apply at all, or at least do not apply in the same sense, to the judgements that constitute our techniques of description. Our practice of describing the world in language is simply a phenomenon of human history. The techniques of description that have been developed are no doubt conditioned by the nature of the creatures who use them and by the nature of the environment they inhabit. But the relation of our practice to these facts is to be understood as akin to the relation between a species and an environmental niche, and not in terms of mirroring or matching. These techniques are the ones that have proved themselves.

In chapter 6, we discussed four ways in which knowledge claims involving Moore-type propositions allegedly fail to meet implications that are carried by our ordinary use of the words 'I know'. It is perhaps worth returning to these points briefly, to look at them in the light of the new interpretation of our certainty concerning them. It was suggested, first of all, that knowledge claims involving Moore-type propositions cannot serve the point of an ordinary knowledge claim, in so far as either these judgements are already common property, or they will be accepted without doubt, as judgements for which the question of evidence or expertise does not arise. It is now clear that the reason we cannot put forward Moore-type propositions as evidence-based information, or expert knowledge, is that these are the judgements that competent speakers either share or which they may affirm authoritatively, in virtue of their mastery of the practice. We may affirm Moore-type propositions in the course of introducing others to a part of the frame they do not yet share (e.g. 'My name is M. McG.'), or in the course of teaching a child the language, but in these cases we are either extending the framework within which our hearer operates, or we are instructing him in how the words of our language are used. Acknowledging someone as a master of of the language entails (consists in) treating him as someone who will make certain judgements as a matter of course, and who will be willing to accept others as beyond question or doubt. We cannot meet the implication of special information or expertise in the case of Moore-type propositions because it is in the nature of our practice that these judgements should be ones that we either share or which speakers may affirm authoritatively, simply in virtue of being competent members of the practice.

Wittgenstein's second criticism of the philosopher's use of the words 'I know' argued that the implication that one can state how one knows, give the grounds of one's knowledge claim, cannot be met in the case of Moore-type propositions, in so far as we cannot properly understand the notion of grounds in connection with them. Thus, our certainty concerning these propositions is held by Wittgenstein to represent 'the rock bottom of our convictions'; we could not be more certain of anything than we are of them. What we can say now is that the peculiar certainty of Moore-type propositions is not to be understood as the furthest point on a scale of epistemic certainty, which begins with hesitant opinion and ends with conviction that certain things are so. It is not that one is 'trying to express . . . the greatest subjective certainty, but rather that certain propositions seem to underlie all questions and all thinking' (OC, 415). We are not to think of certainty here as 'merely a constructed point to which some things approximate more, some less closely. No. Doubt gradually loses its sense' (OC, 56). Where doubt loses its sense we have 'not certain propositions striking us immediately as true', but 'an ungrounded way of acting'. The certainty of Moore-type propositions is the practical sureness that comes with mastery of the language. There is no space for the notion of grounds to squeeze in because affirming these propositions is a matter of the immediate exercise of linguistic capacities, and not a matter of forming or expressing opinions. Wittgenstein attempts to capture the essential point at OC, 510-11 as follows:

> If I say 'Of course I know that that's a towel' I am making an *utterance*. I have no thought of verification. For me it is an immediate utterance.
>
> I don't think of past or future. (And of course it's the same for Moore too.)
>
> It is just like directly taking hold of something, as I take hold of my towel without having doubts.
>
> And yet this direct taking-hold corresponds to a *sureness*, not to a knowing.
>
> But don't I take hold of a thing's name like that, too?

The third criticism suggests that saying 'I know' is to treat the embedded proposition as an hypothesis, and argues that we cannot create the required epistemic distance between ourselves and Moore-type propositions. Likewise, the fourth criticism argues that we cannot properly understand what it would be to turn out to be wrong about these propositions. Both of these points can now be better understood. The epistemic distance that is essential for the concepts of hypothesis and mistake to make sense is lacking because these judgements express the practical sureness of someone who has mastered the techniques of our linguistic practice. The idea that being overturned in these judgements would mean that one 'lost one's footing completely' is, therefore, to be taken quite literally: it is one's ability to *act* – i.e. to *use* the language – that would be undercut, and we would be plunged into pre-linguistic chaos or void. And if there is no guarantee that this overturning will not happen, the absence of such a guarantee need not effect me. I simply continue to do what I have always done anyway, quite independently of reason: live and act in the ways that my nature and my training have made inevitable to me. The important point, of course, is that this cannot be construed as dogmatism on my part, for the question of justification for living as I have always done, when nothing has occurred to trouble me, simply does not arise.

The account that Wittgenstein has offered of our certainty regarding Moore-type propositions also puts us in a position to diagnose precisely the failures of both the sceptic's attempt to doubt and Moore's claim to know them. Moore's knowledge claims inevetably have the effect of presenting propositions that have, in the context, the role of determining the meaning of our words, as if they were empirical judgements, things which we claim on the basis of evidence, whose truth or falsity must be determined. By presenting Moore-type propositions in this light, Moore's claims merely serve to bring out that these propositions do not have any special epistemic status. Used as empirical judgements they are just as much in need of being established, and just as much open to doubt, as any other empirical judgement we express. It is for this reason, of course, that Moore's subsequent refusal to hearken to the sceptic's doubt is, by the principles of our ordinary language-game, a piece of unacceptable dogmatism. Indeed, the equally unsatisfactory alternatives of doubt and dogmatism become inevitable as soon as Moore takes the step of misrepresenting our relation to 'This is a hand', in a context in which it functions as a technique-constituting judgement, as an epistemic one.

The essential failure of the sceptic's attempt to doubt Moore-type propositions can now also be more clearly understood. First of all, we can see that the sceptic's inability to live his doubt is made inevitable by the role that Moore-type propositions play in the practice, or form of life, that has become his own. Commitment to Moore-type propositions is constitutive of abilities which are entrenched in everything we do and say and think. To put off this commitment would be to cease to describe, to see, to react to, and to act on the world in the ways that have become natural to us. More importantly, Wittgenstein's account of our relationship to Moore-type propositions now allows us to see why the sceptic's doubts are, on the one hand, misplaced, and on the other, incoherent. The sceptic's doubts are misplaced for precisely the same reason that Moore's knowledge claims are: *His doubts misrepresent our relationship to propositions that are, in the context, technique-constituting propositions and treats it as an epistemic relation to empirical judgements.* Our certainty concerning these propositions is not an unjustified presumption of knowledge of truths, which the sceptic exposes, and then seeks unsuccessfully to remedy. It represents, rather, our practical mastery of techniques of description which we perpetually employ in the course of our everyday lives. The question of justification is not neglected but irrelevant: our authority as masters of the practice is all the basis required for our commitment to these propositions.

At the same time, Wittgenstein's account of the role of Moore-type propositions reveals the sceptic's attempt to question them as incoherent. The discussion of rule-following which, as we have seen, underpins his rebuttal of the sceptic, establishes that there exists a language just in so far as there exists a practice of employing expressions, or form of life. Speaking meaningfully, therefore, means speaking within a practice. And speaking within a practice means speaking within the framework of judgements that constitute the techniques of description, or customary way of employing expressions. Thus, an attitude of commitment to Moore-type propositions is a conditon of the meaningful employment of the expressions of our language. The sceptic cannot replace commitment with an attitude of questioning without destroying the meaning of the expression (the techniques of description) in terms of which he tries to express his enquiry. Thus, whatever residual sense we had that we do not fully understand the sceptic's attempt to doubt that the object before him is a hand, is now revealed as a form of practical perplexity: Isn't this precisely what we call 'a hand', precisely what a hand *is*? 'If I wanted to doubt whether this was my hand, how could I avoid doubting that the word "hand" had any meaning?' (OC, 369). 'If . . . I doubt or am uncertain about this being my hand (in whatever sense), why not in that case about the meaning of these words as well?' (OC, 456).

Wittgenstein's exposure of the riddle of scepticism works, therefore, by providing an account of the nature of the judgements that form the frame of our practice, an account that allows us to see why the sceptic's sense that justifications are needed for them is fundamentally erroneous. The great strength of his rebuttal of the sceptic lies in the fact that it provides a genuine resolution of the tension between the unanswerability and the unliveability of scepticism. On the one hand, he has shown how the workings of our language-game make the sceptical argument inevitable, once the step or treating our relationship to the judgements of the frame as an epistemic one has been taken. On the other hand, he has revealed why the sceptic's argument is completely powerless to affect our conviction concerning these judgements. Our certainty regarding them is of a sort that cannot feel the call for justification as a genuine need. It is a practical certainty, a confident 'taking hold', which does not spring from the possession of good reasons, but is an expression of our accomplishment in the employment of our techniques of description. The approach does not attempt to tackle scepticism by undertaking the impossible – and entirely misconceived – task of proving that our world view is certainly correct. But nor does it depend on our dogmatically accepting Moore-type propositions as certainly true, without proof, in order to reveal the emptiness of the traditional enquiry. Rather, it shows why the concepts of truth and falsity, and all epistemic concepts, cease to apply at the level at which our techniques for describing the world are constituted. Our commitment to the judgements that form the frame of enquiry is not a matter of unexamined presupposition that certain things are so but a practical commitment to the employment of techniques which alone give us the power of thought and meaningful expression.

What I am arguing, therefore, is that Wittgenstein does indeed provide the philosophical understanding that I have all along suggested is crucial to a philosophically satisfactory rebuttal of the sceptic. He provides an understanding of what the absence of justification for the judgements of the frame means that does not lead to the sceptical assessment of our ordinary practice. He allows us to see why our ordinary sense that justifications for these judgements are not required is entirely correct, and why in not supplying justifications we are not failing to do something that is needed. Wittgenstein is not using the hold that ordinary practice has on us as the basis for a dogmatic rejection of the sceptic. He is providing a philosophical understanding of what lies at the foundation of ordinary practice that shows that the sceptic's assessment of the judgements of the frame is out of place and incorrect. Thus something of significance has been learnt through the contemplation of the possibility of constructing a sceptical attack on ordinary practice, and of the impossibility of our feeling the attack as any sort of genuine threat. For Wittgenstein, these two facts combine to reveal the true nature of the judgements that form the frame of our practice, and of our certainty concerning them.

Earlier, I argued that Moore's Proof should be seen as an argument from the inability of scepticism to bring conviction that our ordinary judgements and knowledge claims are false or unwarranted, to its complete intellectual bankruptcy. I suggested that the ambivalence we feel concerning the Proof arises because it makes us feel the tension between the unanswerability and the unliveability of scepticism. On the one hand, we cannot but recognize that we share Moore's conviction concerning the judgement 'This is a hand'; on the other, we cannot but feel that, while the sceptical argument remains unanswered, he has no right to affirm it. Moore's Proof was seen as unsatisfactory in so far as it does nothing to earn the conviction that we ordinarily feel concerning the judgements that he takes as premises to his Proof. He does not show why his inability to justify these judgements to the sceptic's satisfaction is not a failure on his part. Looking back at the Proof now, we are in a position to understand the undogmatic base of Moore's sureness that the object before him is a hand. Wittgenstein's account of the nature of our relationship to Moore-type propositions allows us to see why Moore's commitment to the judgement, 'Here is one hand and here is another', does not stand in need of a justification. The essential philosophical work that Moore neglected has been done, and our ambivalence about the Proof can now be fully understood.

Similarly, the account of our practice of using language that Wittgenstein has offered allows us, not only to see why Austin's method for discovering what the phenomenon of knowledge is is correct, but also to motivate the method of linguistic phenomenology in general. It is our practice of employing words that determines our techniques of description. This practice is systematic, in the sense that our techniques of description interact with one another in such a way as to produce either sense or nonsense. The exploration of the boundary between sense and nonsense, or between descriptions that we could and could not use, or between what we should and should not say, is the exploration of the grammar of our techniques. In so far as our techniques determine what, or what kind of thing, it is we are talking about, the grammar of our techniques is likewise the grammar of the phenomena. We find out 'the grammar of objects' through the careful articulation of the ways in which our techniques for describing the world interact. The 'truths' that this investigation throws up are not empirical but timeless, *a priori* propositions that reveal what is essential to our thinking of anything as a chair, as a pain, as a claim to know a proposition, or as an intentional action; they show us what a physical object, a mental state, knowledge, or an action is. It is perhaps unsurprising, but none the less striking, that Austin's investigation of 'what we should (and shouldn't) say when' reveals precisely the grammatical connection between the notions of knowledge, grounds, hypothesis and mistake that Wittgenstein's investigation of the language-game of epistemic concepts also exposes.

Finally, I argued in chapter 5, that Cavell shows only that, from within the perspective of common-sense engagement, we do not feel a need either to affirm or to justify the judgements that constitute our common poperty as speakers of the language, and that we would not, within common sense, find anyone who did feel a need to affirm or to justify these propositions intelligible. Wittgenstien's account of our relationship to Moore-type propositions has now illuminated the precise nature of our shared, common-sense conviction in the judgements of the frame, and the exact source of the unintelligibility involved in putting them forward as knowledge claims. The account allows us to understand what Cavell left unexplained, namely, why it is that we can 'feel content' with our ordinary attitude. The non-sceptical interpretation of the absence of justification for the judgements of the frame, and an account that reveals why our ordinary conviction is neither presumptuous or dogmatic, have, I believe, at last been provided.

Bibliography

Austin, J. L. 1962: *Sense and Sensibilia*, Oxford University Press.
    1961: 'Other Minds', in J. L. Austin, *Philosophical Papers*, 1st edn, Oxford University Press, pp. 44ff.
    1961: 'A Plea for Excuses', in J. L. Austin, *Philosophical Papers*, 1st edn, Oxford University Press, pp. 123ff.
Cavell, S. 1979: *The Claim of Reason*, Oxford University Press.
Clarke, T. 1972: 'The Legacy of Skepticism', *Journal of Philosophy*, pp. 759ff.
Davidson, D. 1984: *Inquiries into Truth and Interpretation*, Clarendon Press.
Descartes, R. : *The Philosophical Works of Descartes*, 1st edn (2 vols, 1967), vol. 1, trans. E. S. Haldane and G. R. T. Ross, Cambridge University Press.
Furberg, M. 1971: *Saying and Meaning: A Main Theme in J. L. Austin's Philosophy*, Basil Blackwell.
McGinn, C. 1983: *The Subjective View*, Oxford University Press.
Moore, G. E. 1963: 'Proof of an External World', in G. E. Moore, *Philosophical Papers*, Allen and Unwin, pp. 127ff.
    1970: 'Hume's Philosophy', in G. E. Moore, *Philosophical Studies*, Routledge and Kegan Paul, pp. 147ff.
Nagel, T. 1986: *The View From Nowhere*, Oxford University Press.
Stroud, B. 1984: *The Significance of Philosophical Scepticism*, Oxford University Press.
Williams, M. 1971: *Groundless Belief*, Basil Blackwell.
Wittgenstein, L. 1971: *Tractatus Logico Philosophicus* (TLP), Routledge and Kegan Paul.
    1972: *Philosophical Investigations* (PI), Basil Blackwell.
    1974: *Philosophical Grammar*, Basil Blackwell.
    1977: *On Certainty* (OC), Basil Blackwell.
    1978: *Blue and Brown Books*, Basil Blackwell.
    1978: *Remarks on the Foundation of Mathematics* (RFM), Basil Blackwell.

Index